Day in,

Day out

The 2004
Christian Companion

Day in, Day out
Published by Foundery Press

© Trustees Methodist Church Purposes, 2003

Cover picture photography:
    © 2002 Creatas, Time Icons

ISBN 1 85852 243 9

Compiled by Susan Hibbins

Printed by Stanley L. Hunt (Printers) Ltd

CONTENTS

FOREWORD

If I were to be granted three wishes for the Church, I think I know what one of them would be. I should wish for the Church – that is, for every Christian and would-be Christian – the gift of continual prayer.

St. Paul commended it: 'Pray without ceasing', (1 Thessalonians 5:17). Some Christians, like Brother Lawrence, the monk who worked for 30 years in the monastery kitchen and who, by his example, taught 'the practice of the presence of God', have done just that. Thomas Kelly, a 20th -century American from the Quaker tradition, discovered the same inward wealth. At first, he says, prayer is a matter of alternating between outward things and 'the Inner Light'. But the aim is worship 'undergirding every moment', the kind of prayer which is 'the continuous current and background of all moments of life'.

Is that beyond our reach? Not at all! Brother Lawrence and Thomas Kelly – and many more – would be the first to encourage us on!

What else might I wish for us all? It would be the 'discipline' (if that's the right word) of what used to be called 'spiritual reading'. Think of all the things we can read almost every single day: newspapers, periodicals, 'junk mail' advertising cheap holidays, bargain sales and the like . . . there is no end to it! The question is whether we can, or will, make space for something different.

The Bible, of course, would be a vital part of our spiritual reading, but so would other books – the kind which prompt us to think about life, our faith and God. Or, to put it another way, the kind of books which help us to pray, and so to cope with life rather better than we would if we didn't read them.

Why do I wish these things for myself and for every would-be follower of Jesus? It is because Christian formation is so urgent and vital 'for the living of these days'. But there are so many pressures on us, (social, economic, cultural), that Christian formation is not something which is going to happen automatically. We need time and space for reflection, reading and prayer.

So regard this book as a gift, and allow the book to become part of a discipline which helps you in your prayers, and in the daily adventure of following Jesus Christ. It is a treasure trove of wisdom, challenge and encouragement, from a wonderful variety of people. It is a resource which can help us to live more fully the life of faith, hope and love to which we are called. Let it be what it offers to be: a companion for your journey, not least, but not only, when the going gets rough.

I pray that *The 2004 Christian Companion* will be widely read, and a source of blessing to all who dip into its pages.

Neil G. Richardson
President of the Methodist Conference, 2003-2004

Awake, awake to love and work . . .

Praying Day in and Day out

Agatha Mary, SPB

In a previous volume of *The Methodist Companion* I found this quotation from Henry Emerson Fosdick: 'Church service really begins on Monday morning at seven o'clock and lasts all week. Church service is helpfulness to people; public worship is a preparation for it.' The present *Companion* is entitled *Day in, Day out*. It has seemed to me for a very long time that what happens on Sundays and what happens in the next six days is really all of a piece. We soon learn in life that many different people, things, circumstances, hopes and fears make up what we call experience; and for anyone who takes Christian faith seriously, the way God is to be sought and found in our daily life is of vital importance.

Looking back, I don't think that I got anywhere near to understanding this very important fact until I started working. That began at the same time as the Second World War and my first job was in the newspaper world of Fleet Street, so I was faced with challenges from the start. There was a life of routine which was made up of changing news and views, plans and strategies, challenges to conscience and faith. My second job took me to the world of writers and publishers with a rather

3

different set of news, views, plans and strategies; and still the challenges were there. All of this was against the background of wartime conditions – the struggle to get to work, rarely knowing if the quickest route was going to be clear or had been bombed overnight, trying to get adequate food after rationing came in, never knowing if the house was going to be intact when I got home (fortunately, I was there when we were bombed), never knowing which of my family or friends would be the next to suffer, being loved and then jilted. It was against this background that I learnt to keep God central to my life; and I found that I could do so in the same way after the war, in the 11 years that I had among the homes and streets of Soweto and other Black areas in South Africa.

After I had been about a year in the convent where I now am, I was asked if I had found the nuns' way of life very different from what I had known previously, and I remember saying, 'Oh no, it's what I was used to; it's all the same.'

The more I think about it, the more I realise that my life's experience has been in so many ways like that of the Wesleys – always busy, going from one thing to another (yes, even within a convent!), facing uncertainties but trying to make plans, doing the next thing that presents itself as needing to be done and struggling to keep in touch with God through it all.

> Prayer is the soul's sincere desire,
>   Uttered or unexpressed;
> The motion of a hidden fire
>   That trembles in the breast.
>
> James Montgomery

In this article I want to look at the different aspects of prayer as I know it, and the way in which it can be applied to daily life. I don't think there is one set way of praying; I include a bit of everything. There is spontaneity in prayer, but there is also effort. St. Paul's injunction in 1 Thessalonians 5:17 has been inhibiting for many of us, instead of encouraging, especially if we were brought up with the translation of the Authorised Version: 'Pray without ceasing.' Modern translations are much more helpful: 'Pray continually' or (better still, to my mind) 'Pray constantly.' Each of these phrases suggests greater freedom. I like 'constantly' best of all because it has overtones of going back to something again and again. And the essence of prayer as I know it is a going back to God, making him a constant point of reference in our lives in the same way as the ones we care about become constant points of reference in our lives – more than that, they do so in very many different circumstances. It is the varieties of forms of prayer that are so exciting.

I want to think, like Fosdick, about the Sunday service, and how our prayer there affects our life of service to others. And for the sake of simplicity, I am going to use words from a hymn of Charles Wesley as God's message-for-the-week:

Forth in thy name, O Lord, I go,
My daily labour to pursue;
Thee, only thee, resolved to know
In all I think, or speak, or do.

During services we take part in praise and teaching, and afterwards we try to live by the gospel values in our interaction with the lives of others. We proclaim the gospel more by what we do than by what we say. This is where the example of Jesus helps us. People believed what he said because of what he did.

St. Luke is our best help in discovering what that was. Chapter 3:23 to chapter 21 of his Gospel describes the ministry of Jesus: teaching, social criticism, challenge, proclaiming good news, sometimes of necessity distancing himself from family pressure, performing miracles, healing, sending others out to preach and heal, welcoming interruptions even when he was praying, warning, meeting people where and as they were, being prepared to face challenges to himself, becoming more and more courageous, calling some to follow him, encouraging, answering questions (even personal questions), noticing changing situations and responding appropriately. This is a long list and many of these activities were undertaken again and again. It is the example that Jesus set us: 'Follow me' (Luke 9:59). We follow as best as we can, according to our character and circumstances.

We can only do what our abilities and opportunities make possible. But we can do that in the strength of the assurances that Jesus gave to his first followers and what St. Matthew records at the end of his Gospel: 'Go, therefore and make disciples of all nations . . . teaching them to obey all that I have commanded you. And remember, I am with you always, to the end of the age' (Matthew 28:19-20).

Jesus, confirm my heart's desire
  To work, and speak, and think for thee;
Still let me guard the holy fire,
  And still stir up thy gift in me.

Charles Wesley

We need to keep close to Jesus through the day, or there can be little opportunity for him to direct us. The more we keep close, the more we shall naturally *do good* as he would have us do. The more our personal prayer grows in depth, the more we shall keep close to other people with their needs and problems. To find Jesus, we have to enter those needs and problems, strange as that may seem. To find Jesus, we have to enter our own selves too, with our needs and problems. This is a very important aspect of prayer and it can take place at any time and in any place.

Prayer is being in relationship with God. All relationships involve a reaching out. God reaches out to people. Our reaching out to him is an act of hope that contact can be made, and as contact begins then recognition of him begins to dawn. This was St. John's experience in the half-light before sunrise at the lake one morning after the resurrection: 'It is the Lord!' (John 21:7). Our responses to the recognition might be amazement, immediate action, praise, humility or gratitude. Whatever our response, it is a deepening of our prayer. And again, it can take place at any time and in any place.

Thee we would be always blessing,
Serve thee as thy hosts above . . .

Charles Wesley

Becoming more and more aware of the presence of God in every part of life, in matters great and small, is a great liberation from the self-centredness that can characterise our lives. Awareness is one of the many gifts that he gives us as our relationship with him develops. We respond to all the demands of daily life with an easier spirit because we know that he is there in it all with us.

But sometimes we are not aware of him. There are two reasons for this. One, which is so often referred to in the Bible, is the fact that God for his own reasons does not make himself known (think of Jesus with the two disciples on the road to Emmaus, described in Luke 24:13-35). God has his own agenda in the same way as we have ours. The other reason for our unawareness is that we ourselves may be so overwhelmed with trouble that all our thought, imagination and feeling has to be poured into the situation facing us. Sometimes, as we all know, such times may be long. But God does not withdraw because our eyes are not on his. He does not leave us, indeed he cannot do so. He remains with us and he loves and strengthens us. At such times when it seems we are not praying – the interaction with God is still going on.

There is another kind of prayer, when God seems to deflect us from what we are doing in order to show us something he wants us to notice. This morning the preacher talked to us about what she called 'the ministry

8

of the prod'. We walk down the street to the shops, passing any number of pedestrians, and suddenly we notice a tender gesture to someone who is disabled or a smile of sheer contentment in a passer-by – and we realise that we have seen the goodness and beauty of God made manifest. We pass a florist's shop and there are flowers out on the pavement. Suddenly we notice just one perfect flower – and our hearts are filled with gratitude.

Sometimes it is not sight or sound or any of the senses that stirs us. Thoughts sometimes come briefly into focus. A fleeting idea flickering along the thread between heart and head can stir us to listen carefully to what God is whispering to us. We should stay attentive until it fades and then just thank him for the gift.

Sometimes we find ourselves repeating words or phrases that come unbidden into our consciousness. This is another way in which our hidden God reveals himself. The gift which the great 18th-century hymn-writers expressed is still enriching our prayer today; they put into words the voice of our crying hearts as we reach out to find our God who is always with us. These hymns are not sentimental but are the authentic voice of true prayer; and if we stay with them when they come to us unbidden, our hearts, like theirs, will pray.

God can be so active in our lives if we will let him. He is beyond us and yet he is in us, with us, part of our very being. We sometimes recognise him in others without realising that he is in us as well. So the whole process of praying constantly, day in and day out, is our opening up to him who is within us. His character is love and compassion. That is his gift and his call to us – to live love and to give love.

> Pray, and praise thee, without ceasing,
> Glory in thy perfect love.

Charles Wesley

*Grant us grace, our Father, to do our work this day
as workmen and women who need not be ashamed.
Give us the spirit of diligence and honest enquiry
in our quest for the truth, the spirit of charity in all
our dealings with our fellow workers, and the spirit
of courage and a quiet mind in facing all tasks and
responsibilities.*

Reinhold Niebuhr

There is a river, a sweet, still, flowing river, the streams
whereof will make glad thy heart. And learn but in
quietness and stillness to retire to the Lord, and wait
upon him; in whom thou shalt feel peace and joy, in the
midst of thy troubles from the cruel and vexatious spirit
of this world. So wait to know thy work and service to
the Lord, in thy place and station; and the Lord will make
thee faithful therein, and thou wilt want neither help,
support, nor comfort.

Isaac Penington

*In making our decisions, we must use the brains that God has
given us. But we must also use our hearts which he also gave
us.*

Fulton Oursler

O most merciful
hear my prayer for grace
to be a good workman in thy kingdom;
and when thou hearest,
forgive.

Work in me of thy good pleasure
both to will and to do thy work,
the work thou willest, when thou willest,
as thou willest;
thine own incessant work
of truth, sympathy, healing, joy;
work that speaks, none knows how, nor I,
the tongue of heaven;
and reveals thyself.

Thou, O God, art in love with all thy work;
it flows, it pours, out of thy heart.
In the bounty of thy grace
make me, O Father, an instrument of it;
the thought be thine, the word thine, the deed
    thine,
the glory all thine:
enough for me
the obedience. Amen.

Eric Milner-White

As the earth can produce
nothing unless it is fertilised by
the sun, so we can do nothing
without the grace of God.

John Vianney

It is not only prayer that gives God glory, but
work. Smiting on an anvil, sawing a beam,
whitewashing a wall, driving horses, sweeping,
scouring, everything gives God glory if being in
his grace you do it as your duty. He is so great
that all things give him glory, if you mean they
should.

Gerard Manley Hopkins

God wills to do something quite definite and particular
through us, here and now, something which no other
person could do at any other time.

Emil Brunner

When you rise in the morning, what fills your head?
Are you thinking of food and drink, the pleasures ahead?
Are you planning the work you must do, the labour ahead?
Are you fearful of snares and dangers, the evils ahead?
Are you hopeful of all you'll achieve, the successes ahead?

Let all those worldly thoughts swirl in your mind;
Then let them flush away, like dirt in a river.
Empty your head; let your brain be at peace.
Quietly, calmly, serenely – offer the day to God.

Celtic parable

The vocation of every man and woman is to serve other people.

Leo Tolstoy

Work is one side of life, the other side is worship; our business is to give each its due attention so as to preserve a balanced life.

John Macbeath

14

As I sat for long hours in front of Rublev's 'Trinity' [an icon] I noticed how gradually my gaze became a prayer. This silent prayer slowly made my inner restlessness melt away and lifted me up into the circle of love, a circle that could not be broken by the powers of the world. Even as I moved away from the icon and became involved in the many tasks of everyday life, I felt as if I did not have to leave the holy place I had found and could dwell there whatever I did or wherever I went.

Henri Nouwen

All heaven is waiting to help those who will discover the will of God and do it.

Robert Ashcroft

Into your hands, O God, we commend ourselves this day; let thy presence be with us to its close. Enable us to feel that in doing our work we are doing thy will, and that in serving others we are serving you; through Jesus Christ our Lord.

Uppingham School Prayer Book

Medicine: Profession and Vocation

Peter Howdle

In recent years doctors have been under increasing scrutiny and pressure. This has been partly because of increasing expectations from patients and politicians but also because of the amazing advances that have been made in modern medicine especially during the past 50 years. As a result, there are more pressures on the healthcare system as we live longer and expect to be more healthy. So, tensions arise around the resources available, the need for better communication, both individually and corporately, and the ethical problems that many of these advances pose for us. Added to this there have been some notable failures on the part of doctors where we have been, quite rightly, criticised. For example, the Bristol Children's Heart Enquiry, the Liverpool Retained Organs scandal, and the cases of individual doctors whose behaviour has been deplorable and who have been 'struck off' the Medical Register. All this has led medical authorities and the Department of Health to look critically at the way doctors work. Many new safeguards and supervisory structures have been put in place and the concept of the 'New Professionalism' has emerged.

Despite all this, I am pleased to say that doctors are still trusted. A MORI poll in 1999 showed that the general public trusted doctors to tell the truth 91 per cent of the time, compared with 77 per cent for judges, 23 per cent for politicians and 15 per cent for journalists!

With all this in mind, I have been looking again at what it means to be 'professional'. There are many definitions but the one which appeals to me most speaks of knowledge, skills and behaviour. The concept of a profession:

- First, the value placed upon systematic knowledge and intellect: knowing
- Second, the value placed upon technical skill and capacity: doing
- Third, the value placed upon putting this conjoint knowledge and skill to work in the service of others: helping.

Thus this is summed up in three words: knowing, doing, helping.

If one pursued one's actions according to such values then I think one would truly be acting in a professional manner. Such behaviour has at its core the ideas of service, responsibility and duty. I would suggest that this understanding of professionalism could apply to all of us at one time or another as we each seek to serve, to help, those around us.

To act in a professional manner is not always easy, of course, whether we be healthcare workers, teachers, clergy, volunteers or family carers. Tensions arise between the one who seeks to serve and the patient, client, church member; and also between the individual who serves and any organisation for which they act.

For example, in my clinical practice it is not uncommon to have a patient admitted to the ward who is confused, aggressive, smells of alcohol and is thought to have taken an overdose of sleeping tablets. He swears at the nurses, frightens the other patients and is using a bed which you or I might need. Yet my knowledge and skills must be put to use to help him, such is my professionalism.

I might ask myself, 'Why do I do this?'

Many people will have various answers to such a question. Mine would be based on what I understand by vocation. I remember as a young teenager knowing that when I left school I wanted to train to become a doctor. I supposed I was 'called'. I couldn't give a list of logically argued reasons, it was a feeling that this is what I had to do. Now, I think I understand my calling, my vocation more clearly. For me it is based in my Christian belief; my vocation is part of my calling to be a Christian. So I think I have the answer as to 'why' I do it. I do it because it is my way of trying to behave in a Christ-like way. My vocation, then, is the basis for my professional behaviour. Of course, it isn't always easy. The alcoholic man is still in that bed on my ward, but the challenge is to treat him as Christ would.

So when I am under pressure, when the weight of expectation seems unreasonable, when I ponder on why am I doing this job, I am supported by my Christian hope and God's grace. And they do help me in my ministry of 'helping'.

As we all seek to fulfil our calling, wherever and whenever that may be, it is often in the small things where our help can be most appreciated. It reminds me of an incident several years ago now. I had a patient who had a stroke at a relatively young age. He made a reasonable recovery and had attended the out-patient clinic for follow-up. At one clinic it emerged that he was not only coming to see me but attending two other clinics at two different hospitals. We agreed it was unnecessary so I discharged him, but told him I would write to the other clinics to make sure that satisfactory arrangements were made for him. I did that, and dropped him a line to tell him what I had done. A few years later, he was readmitted to my ward with another problem. He was pleased to see me, and his first words were: 'Hi man, my wife is always talking about you.' The point was that she had been so grateful that I had taken the trouble to write to them, the letter was kept in a special place in the dressing-table drawer. I was embarrassed and humbled. I thought I had been fulfilling my calling in a professional way, treating him properly. They thought it was very special. It is in such small ways that we so often fulfil our calling. It was William Blake who reminded us that 'He who would do good must do it by minute particulars'. Or in Philip Larkin's words: 'We should be careful/of each other, we should be kind/while there is still time.'[1]

I was very pleased to receive a letter recently from a patient to whom I had given some medical advice. She has discerned my vocation, perhaps because she is ordained, but she wrote, 'I suppose it's partly that I have such faith in your professional gifts but also that I find it easier to accept your comments because we start from similar premises about why we're here.'

So I hope that you have understood how I see my Christian belief underpinning my vocation in medicine. I hope, too, that it doesn't appear self-satisfied since then it ceases to be a vocation.

It is not always easy to act in a professional way, as I have indicated, but our model has to be Jesus. Here is a unique man, who always acted in what I have called a 'professional' way. Look at his knowledge and his skills and how he used his knowing and doing to help those in need. A true professional? More than that, he was following his vocation, and look where that took him.

1   Philip Larkin, 'The Mower', Faber and Faber Ltd.

Speak, Lord, for thy servant heareth.
Grant us ears to hear,
Eyes to see,
Wills to obey,
Hearts to love;
Then declare what thou wilt,
Reveal what thou wilt,
Command what thou wilt,
Demand what thou wilt.

Christina Rossetti

O Lord Jesus Christ, give power, wisdom and gentleness to all your ministering servants, all physicians and surgeons, nurses and watchers by the sick, that, always bearing your presence with them, they may not only heal but bless, and shine as lamps of hope in hours of distress and fear.

Church Missionary Society (adapted)

. . . Adam had been refreshed by his long rest, and with his habitual impatience of mere passivity, he was eager to begin the new day, and subdue sadness by his strong will and strong arm. The white mist lay in the valley; it was going to be a bright, warm day, and he would start work again when he had had his breakfast.

'There's nothing but what's bearable as long as a man can work,' he said to himself: 'the natur o' things doesn't change, though it seems as if one's own life was nothing but change. The square o' four is sixteen, and you must lengthen your lever in proportion to your weight, is as true when a man's miserable as when he's happy; and the best o' working is, it gives you a grip hold o' things outside your own lot.'

George Eliot

Being brought up in a family where to have work was considered lucky rather than preordained did not make it likely that I would be happier without it. At 14 I had to start bringing in a wage packet at the end of the week . . . Clocking in at half-past-seven and out at five-thirty after an energetic day at repetitive and trivial jobs (though I imagine they had some importance in the general scheme of things) initiated me into the discipline of work. Such dull tasks as I was put to needed no thought, and so there was little trespassing on my private dreams, a fact which helped me to stick it out.

Alan Sillitoe

22

I sometimes wonder if we are the wallflowers of the great Christian dance of holiness. We are waiting for our 'real' call, for the job or ministry or artistic expression that will tap our untapped creativity and liberate all our gifts when all around us are opportunities to practise the works of mercy. In our homes, in our families, among our colleagues, in our congregations, in our neighbourhoods.

Wendy M. Wright

Every day is a new path on which to strike out, a new vehicle on which to travel, a new source of energy for us to operate.

Fr. Jerome le Doux

Have thy tools ready; God will find thee work.

Charles Kingsley

I feel a commission to work under God for the revival of this branch of his Church [Methodism] – careless of my own reputation; indifferent to the comments of older and jealous men. I am thirty-six. If I am to serve God in this way, I must no longer shrink from the task – but do it. I have examined my heart for ambition. I am certain it is not there. I hate the criticism I shall evoke and the painful chatter of people. Obscurity, quiet browsing among books, and the service of simple people is my taste – but by the will of God, this is my task . . .

William Sangster

Life is a hard fight, a struggle, a wrestling with the principle of evil, hand to hand, foot to foot. Every inch of the way is disputed. The night is given to us to take breath, to pray, to drink deep at the fountain of power. The day, to use the strength which has been given us, to go forth to work with it till the evening.

Florence Nightingale

Great things must be done greatly, with a great purpose, a great mind, a great courage, a great energy, and a great persistent patience.

Elizabeth Barrett Browning

The great composer does not set to work because he is inspired, but becomes inspired because he is working. Beethoven, Bach and Mozart settled down day after day to the job in hand with as much regularity as an accountant settles down each day to his figures. They didn't waste time waiting for an inspiration.

Ernest Newman

In this quiet moment, before the day's claims thrust themselves upon me, grant me strength for what the day will bring. May there be no part of my life shut out from the influence of your spirit.

Bless those whose true worth is unrecognised, those who serve in lonely places; those whose work is dangerous, those whose work is dull.

Grant your special blessing to all those whose sole desire is to serve your kingdom, and to bring glory to your name.

Rita Snowden

Pray as though no work could help and work as though no prayer could help.

German proverb

25

Letter to my God-daughter – chiefly on social work (with apologies to C. S. Lewis)

Claire Wendelken

Dear Su

I am so thrilled that you are going to train as a social worker. People will call you mad, and try to talk you out of it, but as one who has survived 40 years in the profession I can recommend it! You asked me to tell you about the good things and what I'd found difficult so that you could be better prepared for what lies ahead – so here goes.

All the caring professions offer Christians the rare privilege of being alongside people in trouble, bringing Jesus' love and grace to them in their pain, whether it be emotional or physical. Social work offers the special opportunity of enabling people to grow; to grow more capable of managing in their environment; to grow the ability to communicate in their families; to grow by facing their past and resolving it; to grow by owning up to their mistakes and moving on; to grow in their capacity to contribute to their community.

I was all set to become a journalist; then I became a Christian, and God showed me through Bible readings, prayer and words spoken by Christians who had no knowledge of me, that he wanted me to be a social worker. It meant battles with a headmistress who wouldn't write me a university reference, and with my mother who wanted me to read for an English degree first. You've had battles too, with your mother, about how dangerous it is as a profession. At least, thanks to the changes in training, you can now do your degree in social work.

For me, the main joy has been in acting as a channel of grace by praying and seeing God provide for people. In the 1960s and '70s many of the children in care had lost contact with their families. It was wonderful to see answers to prayer that enabled them to get back in touch. Let me tell you about just one of those situations.

Janet* was the elder child of a woman with mental health problems. At 14 Janet, who had been in care since she was six, longed to find the younger brother she remembered, but no one had been able to find out what had happened to him. Her mother had given no details of him before she disappeared. Authorities had been contacted without success. I had done a couple of searches on my own, following very small clues in the file. Reluctantly I agreed to Janet's plan that she should come with me on a trip around the area where she had lived 10 years before, just to see if it would trigger any memories that would help. I prayed that we would find something, or someone, and that she would not be hurt.

We started at the market, a good place for gossip, and stories about people. Janet found someone who remembered the child-minder her mother had used whose name Janet remembered. The child-minder had moved house. No one knew the address, but they described the new place and how to get there. Janet insisted that we go and confirm the address. It took some finding, but eventually we knocked. There was no doubting who it was who opened the door. Although he was two years younger than Janet the family likeness of her brother was powerful. Many might say it was 'serendipity' at work, but there were too many such occasions to call them other than God-incidences, and answers to prayer.

At different times, in answer to prayer for the families with whom I worked, I saw the state provide in ways that were within their legal powers, but well outside the norm. Housing, respite and educational holidays, special school needs, support workers, foster carers with special skills – God was far better than I at finding them all. Partly it was because I worked for an authority that believed in listening to workers and giving them some autonomy, but the major difference always came after I had prayed specifically.

You will be entering a profession that is going to benefit you as well as those you work with. Social work is good for the worker spiritually! There are lots of opportunities to hand on the grace that you have yourself received and to 'serve in love' (Galatians 5:13). If you keep asking God, he also gives wisdom so that you don't get burned out by the demands of others. The biggest danger is that you get so hooked on enabling people, and having the next thing to do, that you lose sight of the need to pray constantly for that wisdom. It is amazing how powerfully demanding bureaucratic compliance can become when you fail to pray about priorities. The alternative temptation of being sloppy administratively because you are being so loving is just as great!

This leads us on to the problem of sin – social work is about working with sin and enabling others to win their battles against it. Cruelty, ill-health, theft, bullying – all are part of the sin of the world. The devil is the father of lies (John 8:44). We may acknowledge that in our heads, but when it comes to working with people, you do not want to believe that they will lie to *you*. A lot of social work is about lies and enabling people to face up to them. Lies about relationships, lies to cover up the past, lies about where someone has been, lies about needs, lies to obtain things, lies about money, lies to Social Security. These may be presented as different perceptions, distortions, manipulation of facts, misrepresentation, or being economic with the truth, but lies in any form can breed hardness of heart in the social worker in response, unless you pray to remain open to hear the truth through the pain.

Of course, your colleagues won't like the word 'sin' – it smacks of judgement rather than discernment. As a Christian, recognising sin is more like doing an inventory of the enemy's forces than about condemnation for wrongdoing. Recognising the different areas of sin affecting anyone's life is a way of assessing how all your efforts may be undermined. If you know where the attacks may come from, you can pray about those danger areas specifically. I think it is for the problems I have encountered in the areas of sin and ethics that I have most valued the Social Workers' Christian Fellowship, where colleagues from across the country have been willing to share some of the difficulties and ethical struggles they have encountered.

The other great bonus for a Christian in social work is the discipline of your faith. The principles of social work are so relevant when you are reaching out to people with the gospel. Social work teaches us to listen to those we encounter. That means shutting up your own presumptions, not completing others' sentences for them, waiting to let them tell you in their own way. It is so important to strengthen people, not to dominate them; to enable them and not impose your solutions.

Remember, Su that, contrary to public opinion, social work often includes the giving of information, but rarely involves giving advice. A good social worker, like a good educationalist, will endeavour to offer the opportunity for people to discover for themselves. One of the crucial skills is that of enabling others to make choices. This can be an act of faith in itself. Some of those you will be working with may not appear capable of making choices at all. Breaking down the choice into small steps or component parts can be a challenge, but it makes it possible for the person to choose for themselves. The social worker's role may be to enable the person to believe that they can make that choice. It is very exciting when someone chooses for the first time.

Of course, there are times when a social worker has to recognise that someone is no longer able to exercise autonomy, and that they will have to have their liberty of choice taken away. What a difference it makes to know that God grants wisdom beyond our own. When service users' families condemn us, we are still accepted by God.

I know you are eager to share your faith, Su. Many think that there will be endless opportunities to share the gospel, as a Christian involved in social work. That may be so when working for one of the many Christian organisations involved in social care. However, for those employed in the public sector, where speaking of *your* beliefs may not be permitted, there are still many ways of sharing your faith. Teenagers often ask why you do the work you do – challenging you to admit you care for them, or that it is just a job.

Relationship failures bring echoes of past parental failures and so much pain – can God accept me if my partner and parents reject me? While there may be no time to answer in detail, it is the social worker's duty to care for the spiritual needs of their clients as well as their physical needs, so prayer and, maybe, referral to others, are important.

God is the most remarkable career manager too. I never envisaged being other than a social worker. Management was not my scene. Through restructuring, a managerial post became available. Despite colleagues' pressure that I should apply, I was unconvinced so I 'put out a fleece' (Judges 6:37). If it was really God's will that I apply for the post, then the most senior member of the department would ask me to do so. This person was so senior I had only ever spoken to her once! Next morning she summoned me to her office and told me to apply for the job. It was a post I held for 10 years. Because it combined management and continuing case responsibilities, while enabling me to take student social workers on placement, it was a very fulfilling professional opportunity. Later, I was offered, without application, a part-time university post; opportunities to be involved in staff training were also produced by the Lord. I look back on a career progression that he has faithfully provided.

Su, you are setting out with God on an amazing adventure. Whatever branch of social care you end up in you will find he is faithful beyond your imagining. He will be with you in dangerous situations, when mental health problems cause people to need your care and your intervention. He will provide both wisdom and resources for those for whom you pray. The answers won't always be what you expect, but when the going gets tough, and it will, you will not be alone. You will hear his voice saying, 'Never will I leave you' (Hebrews 13:5-6).

Enjoy your training; be sure to find time for fellowship (Hebrews 10:24-25), and come and see me when you can. I wish you were not going to be quite so far away. With my love and prayers for your future career.

Your loving godmother, Claire.

1   C. S. Lewis, *Letters to Malcolm; chiefly on prayer*, William Collins, Sons and Co. Ltd Glasgow, 1963.

*   Name has been changed for confidentiality.

O God, our Father, to whom the issues of life and death belong,
preserve us from all ills.
Preserve us in health of body,
that we may be able to earn a living for ourselves
and for those whom we love.
Preserve us in soundness of mind,
that all our judgements and decisions may be sane and wise.
Preserve us in purity of life,
that we may conquer all temptation and ever do the right,
that we may walk through the world and yet
keep our garments unspotted from the world.

And if illness, misfortune, sorrow come to us, preserve us in
courage, in endurance, and in serenity of faith, that, in all the
changes and chances of life, we may still face life with steady
eyes, because we face life with you.

William Barclay

We must not sit still and look for miracles; up and be doing, and the Lord will be with you. Prayer and pains, through faith in Christ Jesus, will do anything.

John Eliot

People go out today to face a life shadowed by vast industrial, commercial and social problems. Life has grown complicated, involved, hard to understand, difficult to deal with . . . There is the danger that always lurks in things – a warped judgement, a confused reckoning, a narrowed outlook. The danger in the places where people toil is not that God is denied with a vociferous atheism; it is that he is ignored by an unvoiced indifference . . . And thus the real battle of life is not the toil for bread. It is fought by all who would keep alive and fresh in their hearts the truth that people do not live by bread alone.

Percy Ainsworth

Early in the morning, I wait on you, O Lord;
Day by day I toil for you, O Lord;
At the bright noon-day I recollect you, O Lord;
In talk and recreation I enjoy you, O Lord;
In study and prayer I learn of you, O Lord;
At nightfall and in sleep, I rest in you, O Lord.

Ray Simpson

Ask God to give thee skill
In comfort's art;
That thou mayst consecrated be
And set apart,
Into a life of sympathy.
For heavy is the weight of ill
In every heart;
And comforters are needed much
Of Christlike touch.

A. E. Hamilton

Help us, this day, O God, to run with patience the race
that is set before us. May neither opposition nor
discouragement divert us from our goal. Inspire in us
both strength of mind and steadfastness of purpose, that
we may meet all fears and difficulties with unswerving
courage, and may fulfil with quiet fidelity the tasks
committed to our charge.

H. Bisseker

For the first few days Laura feared she would never learn her new duties. Even in that small country Post Office there was in use what seemed to her a bewildering number and variety of official forms, to all of which Miss Lane, who loved to make a mystery of her work, referred by number, not name. But soon, in actual practice, 'AB/35', 'K.21', or 'X.Y.13', or whatnot became 'The blue Savings Bank Form', 'The Postal Order Abstract', 'The Cash Account Sheet', and so on, and Laura found herself flicking them out their pigeon-holes and carrying them without a moment's hesitation to where Miss Lane sat doing her accounts at the kitchen table.

Flora Thompson

The analogy I like best of God's upholding is that of the singer and the song. The song depends totally on being uttered by the singer, moment by moment. So it is, I believe, with God and the universe, including humankind. We owe our moment-by-moment existence to the upholding of God.

Colin Humphreys

See your best self – the one surrendered to God, co-operating with him, taking his resources, working out life together, a 'you' loosened from what you have been and done, reinforced with divine energy and insight, a 'you' that does things beyond your capacity, a 'you' poised, progressive, productive.

E. Stanley Jones

Forth in thy name, O Lord, I go,
My daily labour to pursue,
Thee, only thee, resolved to know
In all I think, or speak, or do.

The task thy wisdom has assigned
O let me cheerfully fulfil,
In all my works thy presence find,
And prove thy good and perfect will.

Thee may I set at my right hand,
Whose eyes my inmost substance see,
And labour on at thy command,
And offer all my works to thee.

Give me to bear thy easy yoke,
And every moment watch and pray,
And still to things eternal look,
And hasten to thy glorious day;

For thee delightfully employ
Whate'er thy bounteous grace has given,
And run my course with even joy,
And closely walk with thee to heaven.

Charles Wesley

CHARISMA

Peter Garner

Shortly after I became a Christian I began to read the Bible in a systematic way, memorising Scripture verses to help me in my work as a member of a parish visiting team. Gradually this led me to read the Bible thematically, which helped me to deepen my understanding and my faith.

In due course, the apostle Paul's Letters opened up another strand of understanding, as they appealed to something which greatly interested me: the application of biblical understanding to working relationships and the daily working environment. I was aware of the way in which people reacted to their work, and had observed how periods of disenchantment could affect them, leading some people to leave for other jobs.

While I was making this study of St. Paul, I shared my new-found enthusiasms with a Christian fellow-commuter on my daily rail journeys into London, and it was not long before he invited me to address the London branch of the British Institute of Management (as it was then known) on the subject of Christian Management Principles at Work. At the same time he gave me a leaflet outlining information on Good Management Practice.

It soon became clear to me that St. Paul had a great deal to offer in matters of good working relationships and, equally, that the writers of the BIM Code of Good Management Practice might well have been readers of the Bible – and St. Paul's Letters in particular.

Throughout my thematic studies, I have found it useful to use acronyms to help me memorise things. This certainly helped in developing a workcode programme, and the acronym which emerged was an appropriate one – CHARISMA – a neat link to the concept of the gifts of grace to the body of Christ by the Holy Spirit.

I shall always be grateful for that invitation to address the BIM London Branch as it got me started on a process of study and helped me to develop a Christian relational framework which has always served me well in my desire to help people work together effectively and harmoniously.

It may help if I lay out the eight-point acronym to illustrate the components of good working relationships – but firstly let me mention the chapters of St. Paul's Letters which contain his recommendations for working practice: Romans 12, Ephesians 4, Colossians 3 and Philippians 2.

The CHARISMA code is outlined as follows:

C – Creative Communication
H – Humility and Delegation
A – Accountability to Others
R – Relationships in Unity
I   – Interdependent Attitudes
S – Strengths as Resources
M – Management and Service
A – Ambition in Common Goals

Communication
Everything starts from here. Paul says, 'Be of one mind' – in other words, good communication develops and maintains unity, commitment and motivation in achieving objectives. In fact, communication is the lifeblood of any organisation; without it, a group withers and chaos reigns. Communication is the power or weakness in any grouping, sacred or secular. It needs to be a two-way process, like a radio network which is able to transmit and receive. The organisation which always listens to its workforce, its customers and its suppliers before communicating strategy and products is always likely to be near the top of the league! The Bible is God's way of communicating to us – he created the world and knows its workings just as he understands us. Are we, first and foremost, in touch with him through prayer and reading of his Word?

Humility
This characteristic was exemplified in Christ himself and lies at the very heart of a Christian lifestyle. It will cause us to respect and value everyone with whom we work, lead towards more creative relationships and ensure that

every skill and talent entrusted by God to our colleagues will be invited into action and exercised for the benefit of all. Recognition of the skills of others (on whom we depend) will mark us out as people who know what life, as planned by God, is all about. This applies equally to any church or organisation, and especially to the workplace. Jesus was not a 'one man band' – he chose a team of people and motivated them through humility. Assertiveness is often stressed in current management training – but will not, I believe, be found in Christian teaching. In the long run it is self-defeating and counter-productive.

Accountability

Christians know that everything they have comes from God, and that they are accountable to him for their everyday life and work, and their daily stewardship of time, talents and resources. That vertical accountability leads to a horizontal accountability to all those, senior or junior, with whom we work. We are accountable people and people who take account of the needs, ideas, problems and suggestions of others. Accountability should lie at the heart of our attitudes, actions and achievements. The shape of the cross of Christ, who demonstrated accountability to his heavenly Father and to his fellow human beings – will remind us each day of these vital ingredients in developing constructive attitudes to work.

Relationships

Above all else, Christian faith concerns relationships. Without a relationship with God, through Christ, my efforts towards profitable relationships at work will always founder on the stumbling-blocks of human nature and self-orientation. Personal ambition is committed to promoting self, and will, inevitably, destroy unity. An ability to show genuine interest in and respect for others, combined with that essential ingredient of a sense of humour, cannot fail to increase the harmony of our lives – and of our workplaces.

Interdependence
No one has ever possessed all the attributes he or she needs for total success at work, at church or in family life. It is therefore a good idea to look on others as a vital part of our plans. And, in any case, team spirit helps us to accomplish more than we can by working by ourselves. Jesus taught his disciples to work as a team in order to accomplish a common goal. He recognised the principle of team dynamics – the mutual exchange of advice, assistance and encouragement which will transform the profitability of any enterprise, perhaps starting at the top! Do I depend on others for their part in my objectives? Am I a team person? The best way to discover this is to ask a friend who is brave enough to be strictly honest! Finding independent Christians should be a difficult task – is that true in your experience?

Strengths
Jesus achieved his purposes in a way that was totally opposed to the self-striving of the world. His method is the pattern for the Christian at work. Influence followed obedience and self-sacrifice. This dynamic confounds human logic, but experience always proves its validity. The Christian attitude to potential is grounded in the knowledge that God's infinite resources are always made

available to those who are submitted to his plan and purpose. Our strengths as individuals are only released to the full as we abandon self – the cross is again our illustration of this mystery. Do I recognise that, in God's sight, every person is unique and valuable for what he or she is, rather than for what he or she does? Am I using my skills and perhaps the skills of others effectively, for the benefit of the whole organisation? Corporate strength surely follows when this principle is used, both individually and corporately.

Management
Christian managers know that they are subject to higher authority and this must show – in open attitudes and in a more consultative leadership style. Compassion plays an integral part. Power can be dangerous; do I use it with care and for the good of all with whom I work? Do I seek to serve, rather than to be served, as Jesus did? Accountability needs to match authority – these two go hand-in-hand in Christian management practice. God raised Jesus to the highest place but his 'promotion' was earned through his willing humiliation. He is the Servant King. The servant business leader or manager will be a motivator of people in surprising ways which will be amply revealed if this management style is applied.

Ambition
As a challenge, here are a few questions which will help us to address this next heading. Do I want to succeed so that others will benefit as well as myself? Are my goals part of a corporate or purely individual strategy? Is God at the centre of my motivation and overall perspective?

Ambition outside God's plan for our lives sets aside his sovereignty and demonstrates a disobedient spirit. Christian faith brings with it new aims and objectives – self-seeking gives way to self-sacrifice which, in turn, brings with it surprising results. The Christian Handbook, the Bible, so often neglected and overlooked in its everyday relevance, contains real power for success at work. When we put our ambitions alongside those of the Master Planner, we can expect a different set of achievements.

May the Lord use all his resources to help us to witness to his presence in everyday situations for the extension of his kingdom!

I was overseeing a conference of five people who got into a heated discussion. It was my job to observe the process in order to reflect back to them some of the causes of their office problems. One of the men suddenly said, 'I don't want to talk about it anymore. We're getting nowhere.'

There was an embarrassing silence.

I had an immediate awareness that there was a power present that I couldn't explain. I heard myself saying, 'I have a sense we're on holy ground. And in the midst of the mystery of trying to understand the problem, we're nearly at the resolution and the revelation of it.'

It was odd. I'd never said anything like that before. The others looked at me and seemed to sense something different at that moment as well. A resolution came quickly after that. God's power was at work in my work.

Source unknown

I can picture [Jesus'] style in the workplace – friendly greetings, words of encouragement, going the extra mile for a customer or a colleague. His manner in meetings, on the phone or in the field would be affirming. Dozens of people every day would experience, if only for a moment, a caring person focusing fully on them.

James McGinnin

Christians can easily succumb to this . . . pressure to 'keep the sacred out of the secular'. On the one hand, those who are involved in leadership at work, where they have great expertise in strategic planning, goal setting and team building, may feel that their skills are somehow 'unspiritual' and irrelevant to the life of the church. Simultaneously, a lack of integration can mean that committed Christians fail to live and think Christianly in the workplace, neither applying biblical principles to business ethics, nor finding time to pray. We get sucked into the workaholism of the world, but the pressure may seem even worse for the dedicated believer because we additionally have to squeeze all our church activities into a life that is already far too frenetic.

Rob Warner

A day is a way: it needs direction. A day is a work: it demands definite resolution.

Anonymous

A book existing in the mind is one thing, enclosed there it is delightful company, but when the glow becomes an explosive personality demanding to get out that is quite another. It must be got out, or the writer will go mad, but getting the thing down on paper is a grinding slog. The thought of starting the process yet again fills one with dark despair. Anything not to start . . . I don't know what other writers do in this miserable condition. I only know what I do. Sit down at the appointed time for work and stare in terror at the empty sheet of paper before me. How many of those blank white papers must be covered with hideous black marks before the book is finished? Hundreds of them. But what a crazy way to earn a living, making dirty marks on clean paper . . .

Elizabeth Goudge

Shift your emphasis from problems to challenges . . . When you have problems you worry about them. When you have challenges, you are working, applying and attacking a plan to get results. Don't let your unsolved problems pursue you; make your decisions and forget them, and then do your job as well as you can.

Joe D. Batten and Leonard C. Hudson

The secret of life is to have a task, something you devote your entire life to, something you bring everything to, every minute of the day for your whole life.

Henry Moore

O God,
help me to walk in the boots of
    the miner,
the shoes of the trader, the
    moccasins of the trapper,
and in the sandals of Jesus
    Christ the Master,
and to see others as he would
    see them.

From Canada

I have tried to imagine our Lord in today's world. Would he take long distance phone calls? Would he fly rather than walk? Would he be interested in direct mail campaigns? How would he handle the huge number of relationships that modern technology has made it possible for us to maintain? How would he fit into a time where words spoken can be flashed around the world in seconds to become headlines for the next morning's paper?

Although his world was on a much smaller scale, it would appear that he lived with very much the same sort of intrusions and demands with which we are familiar. But one never gets the feeling . . . that he ever hurried, that he ever had to play 'catch up', or that he was ever taken by surprise.

Gordon Macdonald

48

Rather more than a week later, Edwin had so far entered into the life of his father's business that he could fully share the excitement caused by an impending solemnity in the printing office. He was somewhat pleased with himself, and especially with his seriousness. The memory of school was slipping away from him in the most extraordinary manner . . . He no longer wanted to 'play' now. He despised play. His unique wish was to work. It struck him as curious and delightful that he really enjoyed work. Work had indeed become play. He could not do enough work to satisfy his appetite. And after the work of the day, scorning all silly notions about exercise and relaxation, he would spend the evening in his beautiful new attic, copying designs, which he would sometimes rise early to finish.

Arnold Bennett

Health enough to make work a pleasure.
Wealth enough to support your needs.
Strength to battle with difficulties and overcome them.
Grace enough to confess your sins and forsake them.
Patience enough to toil until some good is accomplished.
Charity enough to see some good in your neighbour.
Love enough to move you to be useful and helpful to others.
Faith enough to make real the things of God.
Hope enough to remove all anxious fears concerning the future.

Johann Wolfgang von Goethe

Dancing for God

Cathy Sincock

This article comes at a pivotal time in my life. I've come to a crossroads where, as a dancer, my future direction needs to be addressed. Decisions are looming regarding marriage, children and future vocation. It is a time when my faith is vitally important. My focus is on faith and life decisions, on practising my faith. I want this article to impart something of what I have learnt to this point. I know little about any other subject other than myself and dance. I never generally enjoy sharing my inner self; my upbringing taught me not to talk about myself too much as it is arrogant and self-indulgent. However, that is really what I know most about and I would feel a fraud trying to convince you of anything else. I'm hoping that God will impart some revelation both to me as the writer and you as the reader.

Springs Dance Company is a professional Christian dance company, formed in 1979. The company responds to invitations to teach and perform in schools, churches, theatres, festivals, conferences and prisons. When I joined in 1997 it was like leaping onto a very fast treadmill. I thought I was there to dance. Before I knew it I was 'communicating the gospel through dance' and teaching people about the 'biblical foundations for dance in the church'. I felt such a fraud. I had never really understood the Bible; in no way was I qualified to teach from it. The way my father had animated Bible stories and characters had made them into good bedtime stories, but that was about my limit. I was stuck at what Gerard Hughes describes in *God of Surprises* as the 'institutional stage'.

I lacked an awareness of what I had to offer the company and struggled with meeting people's 'hunger' for revelation and wisdom. Despite spending a lot of time observing and thinking about life and God, I'm a natural introvert and reserved in sharing my thoughts. Ironically, my job involves performing in front of thousands of people so I began drawing on those inner thoughts and observations and praying very hard.

Like any journey I need to begin at the beginning for the present to make sense and have relevance. My grandfather was a Methodist local preacher; my father is a Methodist local preacher so, inevitably, my upbringing was in the Methodist Church. I have lots of memories of going to church, from Dad promising us mint humbugs if we would just sit still for another five minutes, to the anticipation of demolishing the dregs of Communion wine as we cleared up the odd little thimble glasses. There were times when I performed as part of anniversary services – I was just dancing, but to those watching God was communicating.

One particular Sunday in church, I stood up to sing the final song, before I could go outside and run some laps around the church building. As I stood I felt an intense warmth run rapidly through every vein in my body and a voice so audible I thought the preacher was still talking. I looked round to see if others were showing signs of this same feeling. The prodding finger at my heart and the words were so clear it could have been the man from the national lottery saying, 'It's you, I want you now.' But what do I need with God, I thought; I'm 14, I don't need God. But it seemed that I did, and accepting God into my life was my first step of faith. The next day I felt transformed; I felt like an astronaut walking on the moon, like Zebedee with springs on his feet. My inherent irritability had gone and my viper tongue was stilled.

At this point I was at a relatively critical time in terms of dance exams. I often danced in my bedroom and, in my own way, prayed to God through dance. Romans 8:26 seemed written for me: 'Likewise the Spirit helps us in our weakness; for we do not know how to pray as we ought, but that very Spirit intercedes with sighs [movements] too deep for words.' I remember to this day one particular prayer when I bargained with God, saying that if he helped me pass a particular exam I would dance for him. Although I did not really know what I was saying, I know I prayed it earnestly with my whole heart. That night I had a vision of myself dancing in front of thousands of people. Dancing for God.

Now we skip a few years. At the end of training at a prestigious stage school in London, I scanned *The Stage* searching for a 'decent' dance job. After wading through countless opportunities for lapdancers I found a vacancy I knew was mine. I went along to the audition, got the job, but turned it down.

Love drew me to Coventry where I drifted away from God. I grew tired of training and within the next three years auditioned only twice. Each time I was offered a job, and each time I turned it down. Until one day, when I had been temping for six months, I picked up *The Stage* once again and there was 'my job' with the Springs Dance Company. This time I decided to take it. My first year was a nightmare. I thought I was with a bunch of nutters, that I was being brainwashed. I see it now as a refining, pruning time which continued for a further two years – God had a lot of work to do! I went on to travel the world and dance in front of thousands of people for God, and then I became Artistic Director of the company.

Martin Blogg, one of the co-founders of Springs Dance, has written various books about dance and the Christian faith, and dance and spirituality. He likens the training and journey of the dancer to that of a spiritual journey: times of excelling, times of plateau, times of giving up, the coming down after a high, the struggle, working with others, and being on your own. In terms of my day in, day out faith, what works for me is obedience, part of the discipline of a dancer. My testimony is proof that God's plan will come to fruition. God knows what is right for us; he knows what we are capable of and how much we can take. I relish the fact that in God's creative nature he will find a way for his plans to work out. Maybe it's my upbringing, but I feel I have been blessed with an abundance of faith. I know that faith is an action and we have to practise it. My spiritual journey towards maturity is based on my childlike faith. Just believe and obey!

You will ask where my ideas come from. I cannot say for certain. They come uncalled, sometimes independently, sometimes in association with other things. It seems to me that I could wrest them from Nature herself with my own hands, as I go walking in the woods. They come to me in the silence of the night or in the early morning, stirred into being by moods which the poet would translate into words, but which I put into sounds; and these go through my head ringing and singing and storming until at last I have them before me as notes.

Ludwig van Beethoven

It would seem as if it were a very difficult thing to explain in words, but when I stood before my class of even the smallest and poorest children and said, 'Listen to the music with your soul. Now, while listening, do you not feel an inner self wakening deep within you – that it is by its strength that your head is lifted, that your arms are raised, that you are walking slowly toward the light?' they understood. This awakening is the first step in the dance, as I conceive it.

Isadora Duncan

Self-confidence is the first requisite to great undertakings.

Samuel Johnson

Thou takest the pen – and the lines dance;
Thou takest the flute – and the notes shimmer;
Thou takest the brush – and the colours sing.
So all things have meaning and beauty in that space beyond
time where thou art.
How, then, can I hold anything back from thee?

Dag Hammarskjold

I write about the devout life without being devout
myself, though I certainly desire to be so, and it is my
desire for devotion that encourages me to write . . . I hope
that while I am leading God's beloved sheep to the
waters of devotion, he in his goodness will make my soul
his own.

Francis de Sales

When I think of God my heart is
so filled with joy that the notes
fly off as from a spindle.

Joseph Haydn

Whether you are on the sand worshipping, or at the teacher's desk in a classroom, what does it matter as long as you are doing the will of God?

And if the will of God urges you to seek out the poor, to give up all you possess, or to leave for distant lands, what does the rest matter? Or if it calls you to found a family, or take on a job in a city, why should you have any doubts?

'His will is our peace,' says Dante. And perhaps that is the expression which best brings into focus our deep dependence on God.

Carlo Carretto

Lord, teach us to work with love,
knowing that work is love made visible.
Teach us to weave the cloth with threads
    drawn from our heart,
even as if you our beloved were to wear that
    cloth.
To build a house with affection,
even as if you were to dwell in that house.
To sow seeds with tenderness and reap the
    harvest with joy,
even as if you were to eat the fruit.

Kahlil Gibran

The first day of my new life was a Monday, but the feeling with which I awoke to it was the reverse of that with which Monday mornings are proverbially associated . . . Instead of a fading vision I grasped a clear-cut reality.

Hugh Redwood

Quite often in the summer months, if the tide was early, I would be up at around four or five o'clock making my way down through the town to the Old Harbour. Grandad made no concession to the fact that I was only ten; quite often when the water was low it was necessary to descend a 20-30ft ladder to get down on to the coal barge which was permanently moored and carried all the coal stocks to power the tugs. I had to get down on that and go across several vessels, either tugs or keels, before getting onto Grandad's tug. He always managed to get prime position on the outside of the harbour so he could be first away in the morning. In the harbour there was always a faint hiss in the air – steam being freed from the safety valves on the tugs' boilers, with sometimes a wisp of smoke from the funnels, indicating that the stoker had kept the fire nicely lit all night so that he would have a good head of steam for a start on the tide. Everything tended to be wet or damp, from dew or frost, depending on what time of year it was, and you had to be a bit careful because the decks were made of steel, and it was easy to slip.

Clifford Smith

'Now mind, you have a mistress instead of a master. I don't yet know my powers or my talents in farming; but I shall do my best, and if you serve me well, so shall I serve you. Don't any unfair ones among you (if there are any such, but I hope not) suppose that because I'm a woman I don't understand the difference between bad goings-on and good.'

(All.) 'No 'm!'

(Liddy.) 'Excellent well said.'

'I shall be up before you are awake; I shall be afield before you are up; and I shall have breakfasted before you are afield. In short, I shall astonish you all.'

(All.) 'Yes 'm.'

'And so goodnight.'

(All.) 'Goodnight, ma'am.'

Thomas Hardy

'Miles in the Morning'

Tony Miles

In the beginning was the Word, and the
Word was with God, and the Word was
God.

(John 1:1 NIV)

Beep . . . beep . . . beeeep! Clunk! Without waking,
without a word, my body realises it is 04:02 and my arm
fumbles to switch off the alarm clock. Two minutes later
my mobile lights up and a ring tone plays 'What shall we
do with the drunken sailor?' There's no significance in
the tune (honestly), except that I dislike it so much that
my mind awakes instantly in a desperate attempt to
silence it. The reality dawns that it is 4:02 a.m. and, yes,
it's Saturday . . . again! Surely it can't be, not already.
The third alarm that's set for 04:15 has never been
needed. However, I live in fear that one day there will be
silence, *not a word*, on a Saturday after the 7 o'clock
news on Premier Christian Radio. What, no presenter?

The third security alarm is turned off in time, so that the
rest of the household isn't disturbed. A set routine is
then adhered to on autopilot, *without a word*. This
includes donning clothes, performing all the necessary
morning ablutions, swigging a swift cup of tea and, if I

can face it, making something to eat. Perhaps not! Then I grab my pre-packed satchel and try and leave the house without disturbing the family, the cat, or the other residents of Brook Road. The summer is more bearable, but when it's dark and the car is covered in frost, I have to convince myself of a sense of calling. Thou shalt not covet thy fellow presenters who broadcast at a social hour!

It's surprising how many other people are out and about at 4:30 a.m. The trick is to avoid the speeding milk floats and reckless posties on their bikes. In London, it's amusing to see people still entering and leaving nightclubs! It takes about 45 minutes to drive to Premier's plush new studio in Pimlico; that's three quarters of an hour of news as I channel hop. I find this helps to bring me up to date and to stir the grey matter – the familiar voices of the presenters are comforting and assuring. I listen to a lot of radio. It's a cliché, but the pictures are far better than the television in the theatre of the mind. It's also an activity that can be done whilst doing something else. As I drive and listen, I muster up a prayer or two during the boring bits, or when the news story is over familiar. (I've learnt, however, that it's best not to close one's eyes for meditation when you're driving!) This is my time for telling God things. I'm not yet ready to be receptive to *his Word to me* – perhaps later.

Fortunately there's no congestion charge on Saturdays and parking in London at such an unsocial hour isn't difficult. I ring the 'night bell' to gain entrance to the offices where Premier is located. Being the first to arrive, the security guard is pleased to see me and I look forward to seeing him. We have a polite, but limited conversation – *just a little word.* He knows I'm a Christian and I'm conscious of the opportunity to witness gently. In an hour or so, I shall be broadcasting to thousands of people, all individuals; so my being 'good news' to this person is really important, if the rest of the morning's work is to have integrity. One day I'm tempted to turn up in my 'dog collar', but it might be bit of a shock – a 'Rev' is a bit much to take before breakfast.

Time for action! Just 105 lonely minutes to finalise the show and to *prepare the word* – reading the papers, typing scripts, researching my guests, timing the show to ensure I hit the news on time, scanning emails, checking the music, ensuring that the answers to my competitions are correct, and most important . . . making strong black coffee in the kitchen. The adrenalin begins to rush as 7 o'clock approaches and a few more sleepy Christians join me ready to answer phones for dedications, competitions, and Lifeline's Prayer Team.

I'm now awake! At 6:50 a.m. all those present get together to pray – absolutely essential. John 15:5 comes to mind: '. . . apart from me you can do nothing' (NIV). I will not open the microphone without my prayer time. In the busyness it would be easy to rush in without pausing to make room for God. I recall the words of Jesus to the busy and distracted Martha, '. . . only one thing is needed' (Luke 10:42 NIV). Being against the clock means our devotions are to the point and yet helpful and meaningful. I begin to *receive the Word* myself. I remember that we're there to serve and to meet the needs of our listeners in a variety of ways by *expressing the Word.* We are to be channels of God's love and to make the most of the responsibility God has given us to reach out to people in their homes, cars, work places, prisons, hospitals, or wherever they are. This is a team effort and each person is equally important. It's sobering to remember that I couldn't present the programme without the practical help and prayer support of others. This keeps me grounded. If not careful, being a known personality on the radio can go to your head – even though few people would recognise your face. For the Christian broadcaster, I believe there should be a healthy sense of balance and perspective. For if I try to rely on my own resources and let self take control, I end up distant from God, stressed out and in a mess. I need to draw on the resources of God's Spirit in humility – without whom my witness is in vain and severely diminished.

I have been criticised for becoming involved in what is called 'niche *narrow*casting' rather than *broad*casting. In other words, a Christian radio station is predominantly reaching the converted. This is true. However, I reach more people on a Saturday morning than many ministers speak to in years of preaching and taking services on Sundays. Across all its various platforms (medium wave, cable, satellite and webcasting), Premier reaches over 400,000 people a week – not all are Christians. Yet we don't criticise clergy or local preachers for *preaching the Word* primarily to the converted week by week (perhaps we should!). *Broad*casting and '*narrow*casting' are needed. In the spirit of John Wesley, I simply want to reach and minister to as many people as possible. The question I ask myself is: 'Am I making a positive difference to people's lives and the kingdom?' My experience is 'Yes, by the grace of God.' This is something God asks all his people to do, whatever our calling, or the context of our work.

In my experience, in whatever I do for the Lord, the breath of the Holy Spirit (the Comforter and Enabler) is essential. Deep breathing exercises can be a reminder of this. Then I can be myself and the rest of the programme becomes one unuttered 'four-hour' prayer – harnessing nervous energy by leaning on God with faith. At the heart of all that follows is the 'R' factor – 'Relationship'. That is, my relationship with God first and then my relationship with the listener. We will laugh, cry, learn, pray and worship together. We will enjoy a variety of music, share news, and meet and get to know new friends through my guests on the show. The listener is part of my radio family and he, or she, is deeply loved by God. Radio is a one-to-one relationship and a two-way process. In my radio training, I remember being taught that the word 'communication' comes from the same root as the words 'community' and 'communism'. So for me, 'communication' has come to mean 'making one through the sharing of ideas' – a relationship through *sharing the Word.*

In this aspect of my work, I am reminded that my loving heavenly Father longs to be in relationship with his creation. What's more, God is in the communication business, and by his grace, he reaches out to all humanity, to seek and save the lost, and establish his kingdom.

God, the great Producer and Director,
help me to keep my focus on Jesus,
who was the broadcaster of your word
and also the message.
May I resist the temptation
to become distracted in the performance of my duties.
Rather, let me play my part
in the power of your Spirit of creativity. Amen.[1]

1   © Anthony D. and Frances H. Miles, *Like A Child*,
Rooftops Publishing 2003. Used with permission.

To give and give and give again . . .

The Love of Jesus in Grief

Nigel Lightfoot

She sat opposite me, a woman in the prime of life. One by one each of my questions was answered in a very calm and gracious way. Then, like a bolt from the blue, she answered the last question with a stark realisation that she was now 'Michael's widow'. For Michael was only 34 years old and now, as a result of the ravages of a devastating terminal illness, he had left her and her children alone.

Yet another form lands on my desk and I read that Nellie has died at the age of 78 in a local nursing home. I leave the office and go to another room to meet Arthur and their daughter. 'We were together for 54 years,' he tells me. 'Latterly she did not even know who I was, yet still I went to see her every day. Seems very strange to think that she has gone and left me.'

'Why? Oh, please, will you tell me why?' He was only 13 years old! Life for him had not begun! Robert just did not have a start in life, he struggled from the moment he was born to the time he died. Questions, questions and more questions. Obviously none can be dealt with easily, if at all.

These are cameos of typical situations repeated many times during my working week as a funeral director. I feel very strongly that God not only called me into the work, but that he has equipped me for the tasks and opportunities and daily challenges of the job. I am a person who enjoys meeting and communicating with all sorts of people, those who share my views and those whose opinions, ideas and experiences differ from my own, for this is one of the ways, I believe, in which we are taught tolerance and acceptance of each other. It is within my job as a funeral director that these qualities and many others are needed. People come to see me at a very vulnerable time in their lives. For some it is their first experience of losing a loved one. Some are experiencing anger (which is sometimes levelled at me), others come bewildered, failing to grasp what has happened. Still more come with an almost matter-of-fact approach and seem to have it 'all together'.

Whoever they are and in whatever state I endeavour to exercise my Christian love and concern in the practical way of guiding them through the various tasks which need to be carried out. Burial, cremation, church service or not? Sacred or humanist? Priest or pastor? All and many more different questions have to be asked and answered in order for a funeral to begin to develop; but each thought often brings a tear. Is this really happening?

Amidst all this I am the one who really must keep focused, but at the same time I have to remember that each one is an individual and that all are within God's care. He is there weeping with them just as Jesus did at the tomb of Lazarus, his friend.

My Christian faith, and the fact that I am a local preacher and heavily involved in the life of the Methodist Church, play a very great part in enabling me to fulfil what to many people may seem a very dark and sombre profession. Of course, I know that there is no other job like it. Yet I feel a tremendous sense of privilege to minister in a professional way to people at a very difficult period in their lives. However, within their vulnerability it is not my place to proselytise by setting forth verbally my beliefs and thoughts concerning their situation. At times this can be a little trying as well as a great temptation. Yet over and over again there are times when a small opportunity is given, and some word, some thought can be sensitively given.

When I stop and consider my work, I keep asking the question, what do people expect of a funeral director? I endeavour to maintain and improve upon those requirements, coloured by my own experience and Christian faith. One thing that a client will very soon pick up on is empathy: the fact that you can look them in the eye and they can see your undivided attention, that they really are the only ones that matter in that room. If they recognise that you too have been along the road that they are now travelling; if they see in you one in whom they can confidently trust, then and only then can true help and support be offered and received.

It is at this stage that I have so often been aware that someone else enters the situation. Yes, I would suggest it is an awareness of the Presence who surpasses all our human understanding. And it is not in the form of words, but in quiet, almost indiscernible ways that the

Presence helps us to open up a path forward to allow decisions to be made.

I do not see my profession as a job alone. I feel it is very much a calling. For me as a Christian it holds many challenges which can be turned into opportunities through God's grace working within and through me. Although I deal with death every day, I recognise and rejoice in the recognition that I offer the final gift that can be given to an individual and their family. I consider it is God's plan, for it is an honour to serve society in this way. I am also certain that God uses me, without my knowledge sometimes, to help ease the burden of grief in another, and for that I praise him.

We all have opportunities which come our way from time to time, enabling us to ease another's burden and relieve another's grief. A lot of my job involves sitting and listening. If I fail to listen and hear exactly what is being said I could and would make serious mistakes. People need to share their grief outside the funeral home as well. As the people of God we are called to share one another's burdens. Therefore I would say do not leave it all to the professionals, but take time in your busy schedule to listen and care for the widow and the fatherless. For one day it could be you requiring the undivided attention of another, the helping hand outstretched in your direction, the words of guidance spoken softly to you.

In a secular society such as ours, so clinically orientated, death is the unacceptable part of life. True, it is not easy to accept, yet it is inevitable for all of us for no one is immortal. So just as we rejoice with those who rejoice, let us also take time to weep with those who weep.

When we are willing to abandon ourselves and to fling ourselves outward in compassion and service, we find that we have made room not just for others in our lives but also for God in our hearts. The energy that we had massed in our own little centre is spent on others, leaving an open space where God may enter. From this same God-infused centre also flows the renewing energy that allows us to keep loving and serving in the world. This is why John Wesley affirmed that true faith issues in good works. It is also why Baron von Hugel ordered his spiritual directee, Evelyn Underhill, to serve several days a week in a skid row soup kitchen when she was having trouble with her spiritual life.

True obedience, then, is both a listening to what we hear within us and to what we hear beyond us. It is being attentive to those we encounter in our daily lives. It is creating the empty, open space within us where we can hear God speak.

Thomas R. Hawkins

I am back on night-duty at Camberwell after my leave; in the chapel, as the evening voluntary is played, I stare with swimming eyes at the lettered wall, and remember reading the words: 'I am the Resurrection and the Life' at the early morning communion service before going to Brighton.

I am buying some small accessories for my uniform in a big Victoria store, when I stop, petrified, before a vase of the tall pink roses that Roland gave me on the way to *David Copperfield* . . . and suddenly, to the perturbation of the shop-assistants, I burst into uncontrollable tears, and find myself, helpless and humiliated, unable to stop crying in the tram all the way back to the hospital.

Vera Brittain

> *Comfort the poor, protect and shelter the weak, and with all thy might, right that which is wrong. Then shall the Lord love thee, and God himself shall be thy great reward.*
>
> *Alfred the Great*

My life is hectic! I'm running all day – meetings, phone calls, paperwork, appointments. I push myself to the limit, fall into bed exhausted, and get up early the next morning to do it all again. My output is tremendous; I'm getting a lot done. But I get this feeling inside sometimes, 'So what? What are you doing that really counts?' I have to admit, I don't know.

From an advertisement in *Time* magazine

A life all turbulence and noise may seem
To him that leads it wise and to be praised,
But wisdom is a pearl with most success
Sought in still waters.

William Cowper

In modern life we are dominated by *chronos* [time]. We run our lives, many of us, by diary and clock. We are engaged in a permanent and losing battle against time – losing, because there is never enough of it, and because time by its very nature cannot be 'defeated'. It can only be harnessed and used. It is a very wise prayer to ask, 'Lord, teach me to number my days, that I may incline my heart to wisdom.'

David Winter

If when we plunge our hand
  into a bowl of water,
Or stir up the fire with the bellows
Or tabulate interminable columns of
    figures
  on our book-keeping table,
Or, burnt by the sun, we are plunged
    in the mud of the rice-field,
Or standing by the smelter's furnace
we do not fulfil the same religious life
  as if in prayer in a monastery
the world will never be saved.

                    Mahatma Gandhi

The time of business does not with me differ from the time of prayer; and in the noise and clatter of my kitchen, while several persons are at the same time calling for different things, I possess God in as great tranquillity as if I were upon my knees at the blessed sacrament.

                    Brother Lawrence

At dawn each day she slung her bamboo pole across her shoulder, hooked on the two baskets, jammed her conical basket hat upon her head, and set out barefooted for her garden. As her vegetables ripened, she loaded her baskets and began her long treks through Honolulu . . . When night fell, Nyuk Tsin continued working, putting her field in order, and after the stars had come out she would carefully place in her baskets those vegetables which she had not sold. Swinging them onto her shoulder, she would begin her four-mile trek back up the valley to the clearing where her sons were already asleep.

James A. Michener

It is a mistake to suppose that God is interested solely in religion. God is a worker getting on with his job. He gave [human beings] the joy of creation so that they might share their joy with him.

William Temple

Grabbing the Chance to Speak for Jesus

Gillian Ellis

The Innervation Trust is a team of young people based in Bramhall, Cheshire. Its goal is to flood the UK, Europe and eventually the world with the good news of Jesus Christ by means of up-to-date music, dancing and communication. The vision is to equip schools teams, initially throughout the UK, backed by a fine touring band which will go anywhere, do anything, to support the vision.

The touring band, *thebandwithnoname*, has gone from strength to strength since it was formed early in 2002. Initially the band tackled strenuous tours which proved tremendously successful for its three singers/dancers/communicators Chip, Adam and Bobby. Chip is on fire with enthusiasm as he describes the work: 'D'you know how many kids gave their lives to Jesus on our first 60-date tour?' he says. 'Five hundred! Mind-blowing!'

Manager and producer Mark Pennells and recording expert Zarc Porter are two of the leaders of *Innervation*. Together with the band members, they've come up with an exciting blend of what they describe as 'breakbeat, nu metal and soul'. 'We perform hard-hitting songs with a hard-hitting message,' say the boys. 'The music is out of the ordinary because our message is the most important ingredient.'

The touring band is only part of the story. *Innervation* aims to place schools bands in towns around the UK. Auditions are taking place all over the country for bands which take the gospel message into their local schools, working in assemblies and lessons. Each schools team will be linked to several churches where youngsters who turn to Christ will be nurtured in the faith. The first schools team, an all girl-band, is . well established in Liverpool. In January 2003, *Collective LP* made its debut alongside *thebandwithnoname* at Liverpool's Frontline Church. Since then, it has performed there every month, as well as continuing its schools work.

Touring band singer Chip Kendall, born in Florida, is a lively 25-year-old with a heart for God, an outgoing personality, boundless energy and enthusiasm, an outstanding singing voice and a great sense of humour. Chip's early Christian work included travelling to 25 countries, singing, dancing and making Christian albums. His break came when he had an audition with producer Mark Pennells, and the first *thebandwithnoname* singer was in business.

'Our faith impacts strongly on our work and it's very much a part of what we do,' maintains Chip. 'Unlike other bands, we end all our gigs with a petition. We tell the audience, "We want to give you a chance to respond to the message of Jesus. We'd be doing you a massive disservice if we allowed you to leave this place without giving you that opportunity."

'As a result, we all look deeper into our own faith. Why do we think it's so important for everyone to believe as we do? We've seen loads of kids respond – not that we're only successful if they respond to us, of course! Without a doubt, the gospel message is strong enough to stand on its own. But when we tell the kids about Jesus, it's so encouraging for us to see people turning to him. That just wouldn't happen without our having a strong faith and a desire to see people giving themselves to God.'

How does Chip bring his faith to bear on his daily life? He seizes on the subject eagerly.

'That's a pertinent question for us in a big way. You might think that when Christians work together, everything'll be fine and dandy. In fact, spending all your days with Christians can be an added complication. You want to work well together but you're still human beings who can rub each other up the wrong way. If anything, working together could put us off each other – but that's where our faith comes in. It enables us to have grace and love for each other and to see past things which might upset non-Christians. It's not easy. We really do have to be ready to forgive and not only that, to *forget* about any problems between us. Our faith helps us to forgive, to forget and to love each other, seeing past our human failings to God.'

Chip's work plays a big part in his own Christian journey. He maintains that everyone is on a journey of faith and that nobody can ever say he or she has arrived. That belief has helped him come to grips with dealing with people, whether he meets them often or only once. Faith has helped Chip in his ability to represent Jesus.

The other two members of the band couldn't agree more. Bobby Joel Stearns, aged 25, has been a Christian for as long as he can remember and has always worked in music. He grew up on a 'Youth with a Mission' base in Hawaii, exposed to many different races, nationalities and denominations. In the community setting, he developed a passion for mission and evangelism and felt called to be part of a move to reclaim the music industry for God.

'I remember a preacher once telling me how the Enemy recognises the power of the performing arts as a means of communication and constantly seeks to pervert and distort it. I believe the entire industry is a battlefield and I've always felt a passion to be one of the many dedicated to fight in it.

'Life's empty without God,' Bobby maintains. 'I want to dance and sing to connect kids with God. There is no doubt in my mind that God is doing something really exciting through *Innervation*. There's a growing need to get out there and teach the kids and I'm so glad to be part of it.'

Since leaving university with a Masters degree in Political Science, Bobby has worked with a wide range of artists, writers and producers, as well as choreographing *The Tribe* and *V*enna*, Manchester-based Christian bands. '*Thebandwithnoname* has my name on it, if that's possible!'

he says, enjoying the pun. 'I love the message behind it and it's a privilege to be a part of it, making music for the glory of God and using it to communicate who Jesus really is.'

At 20, Adam Brown, the son of a free church pastor, is the youngest in the touring band. *Innervation* is his first Christian work after college, where he took Media Studies. Adam's 'been there, done that' in the music scene. He was an MC, disc jockey, drummer and bass player in clubs, on Radio One and at big UK events. Working at large church-based gigs sparked a desire to MC with a meaningful content.

'People were totally open to what I was saying over the mike, which gave me a massive responsibility to tell them the truth about God,' he says. 'Over three years working in clubs, I really grabbed the chance to reach people for Jesus.'

Music-lover Adam used to work for HMV by day and as an MC one evening a week in a local nightclub. He voiced his beliefs over the mike in rap and soon, realising he wasn't like the other non-Christian MCs, folks began to ask questions.

'Most rappers go on about sex, drugs or women but you're different,' people would say. Asked about God, Adam delighted in turning his job to Christian advantage. 'There was so much temptation around me but I felt God with me all the time,' he says. 'God gave me a brilliant chance to evangelise where it was really needed. I wouldn't abuse the privilege.'

Adam joined *thebandwithnoname* because he was in the right place at the right time, something which many people might call a coincidence. At *Soul Survivor* 2002, Lindsey, a singer with *The Tribe*, who had heard Adam MC, invited him on stage. 'At the time, a Christian MC was totally unheard of,' says Adam. 'It was exactly what I wanted to do so I wasn't nervous but I sure was excited!'

After that experience, Adam was certain the Lord had something special in store for him. He asked God to show him. 'I know you have a plan for me,' he prayed. 'Show me.'

Shortly after that, driving home one day, Adam was struck by the fact that he cruised through 13 sets of lights at amber. Coincidence? Was he driving at the wrong speed? Somehow, Adam felt it was significant. His mum told him to pray about it. 'I heard God telling me, "Don't go for old opportunities. You've been given many doors to walk through but don't choose yet. Wait. Get ready and keep those revs going." The very next day I had a call. "Mark Pennells here from *Innervation Trust*. I've been given your name by *The Tribe's* Tim Owen. He heard you MC at *Soul Survivor*." '

Mark invited Adam to meet Zarc Porter and to audition. Together they laid down some lyrics then parted company, agreeing to pray about the possibility of working together. A week later, Mark rang again. 'We like you,' he said. 'If it feels right, come and join us.'

Adam's B-TEC in Media Studies has stood him in good stead and he also finds his knowledge of camera work helpful when making music. His faith has a huge impact on his work. 'I really enjoy performing and I know it's God's calling for me. I've never lived just by faith before and God is helping me grow spiritually through it. Away from home for the first time, I'm surrounded by Christians so I always have loads of encouragement. Mark is a father-figure!'

There are stresses, of course: Adam admits to needing his sleep and confesses he gets agitated and bad-tempered when he's hungry. Chip agrees that the band's lifestyle can be exhausting but he offers the ultimate answer: 'When life is stressful and I'm really tired, which is often in our line of work, I remember that the Lord is my strength and song, and I cast my cares on Jesus.'

An Actor's Prayer

My Jesus, bless me in this my actor's life.

Whether I draw tears from an audience or make them laugh, off-stage let me be serious-minded, yet keep my sorrows behind the scenes. May I be undeceived by success and undismayed by failure. Make me generous towards the work of others and a good influence wherever I go. Let me always return to the Sacraments, however often things go wrong.

> On stage, off stage,
> In life, in death,
> Jesus, have mercy
> On my soul.

Denys Blakelock

A Singer's Prayer

Keep me in tune with all thy music, Lord!
Grant me the open mind, the eager heart;
With inner ear to catch thy harmonies
The while I walk with thee in busy mart.

Thread through the quiet grey of common things
The mystic song of beauty, night and noon;
That I may hear thy voice upon the way:
Keep me in tune!

Anonymous

If we are seriously trying to live according to the mind of Christ, we will obviously want to throw ourselves wholeheartedly and with all our skills into our work. We will never be content merely to watch the clock and to regard employment simply as a means to pay the bills and have a good time. There will be legitimate pride in what we do. We will want to master our craft or our profession so as to give greater glory to God.

Basil Hume

I do everything I have to do as if I had only this one thing to do. My divine Love keeps me from any sense of hurry, for in the turmoil of many claims by which I am surrounded I could not keep myself. In every duty I place myself before him as a servant before his master, or a pupil before his teacher, and realise it as his commission. During my work, I talk with him as a friend, I love him and rejoice in him. Even when my work demands my whole attention, my heart is always turned to him.

Armelle Nicolas

Murdstone and Grinby's trade was among a good many kinds of people, but an important branch of it was the supply of wines and spirits to certain packet ships . . . I know that a great many empty bottles were one of the consequences of this traffic, and that certain men and boys were employed to examine them against the light, and reject those that were flawed, and to rinse and wash them. When the empty bottles ran short, there were labels to be pasted on full ones, or corks to be fitted to them, or seals to be put upon the corks, or finished bottles to be packed in casks. All this work was my work, and of the boys employed upon it I was one . . . I felt my hopes of growing up to be a learned and distinguished man crushed in my bosom . . . I mingled my tears with the water in which I was washing the bottles; and sobbed as if there were a flaw in my own breast, and it were in danger of bursting.

Charles Dickens

Creator God, our heavenly Father,
your Son was a carpenter in Nazareth:
we pray for all those who labour in our factories and
    shops.
Grant them wisdom and honesty, strength and skill,
to provide for themselves
and for the needs of our country.
Look with compassion on the landless poor,
the unemployed and homeless,
the orphans and the hungry,
and grant us your power to work towards justice
in transforming their lives for your glory;
through our risen Lord Jesus Christ,
who had nowhere to lay his head.

Kenya

*To watch the corn grow, or the blossoms set; to draw hard
breath over the ploughshare or spade; to read, to think, to pray,
are the things that make people happy.*

John Ruskin

> We do the works, but God
> works in us the doing of the
> works.
>
> Augustine of Hippo

For our Lord to have made a plough from a rotten piece of wood, or to have put up a badly built house, or to have charged an unfair price for his labour, would have been as truly sin as to have yielded ground to the tempter or turned back in sight of the cross. But, because the Carpenter was completely inspired and controlled by creative love, he showed us perfectly how God is always at work in our common life.

J. H. Bodgener

Close by the careless worker's side
    Still patient stands
The Carpenter of Nazareth,
    With piercèd hands
Outstretched to plead unceasingly
    His love's demands.

Longing to pick the hammer up
    And strike a blow
Longing to feel his plane swing out,
    Steady and slow,
The fragrant shavings falling down,
    Silent as snow.

Because this is my work, O Lord,
    It must be thine,
Because it is a human task
    It is divine.
Take me, and brand me with thy cross,
    Thy slave's proud sign.

G. A. Studdert-Kennedy

Faith at the Heart of Pain

Alan Ashton

The small town of Soham in Cambridgeshire was shattered during August 2002. Two 10 year old children, Jessica Chapman and Holly Wells, went missing. A massive search was launched; two weeks later the children's bodies were found, they had been murdered. Two people were arrested and subsequently charged, a service of thanksgiving for the children was held in Ely Cathedral, the private funerals of the children took place. All this happened under the gaze of massive worldwide media coverage – it seemed that in all of this tragedy people wanted to hear the voice of the Church and, as a Methodist minister, I was one of the people who shared in that ministry, sometimes spending all day trying to meet media requests from around the world. August – that 'normally' quiet month for Methodists! – caused me to examine my own faith in the midst of the deaths of these children, the part the events played in my personal Christian journey, as well as the difference the experience has made to the future.

Walk that path with me and find 'faith at the heart of pain'.

Searching

Any walk of faith can involve a search. Just as folk looked for Holly and Jessica, so we need to search to find faith. We need to search and enquire to discover more of what God has to give each of us. It is possible for us to be so busy *being* that we don't stop to search for God. He gets lost under the piles of our various activities. Are we prepared to allow God to search our lives, to examine our motives in the outworking of faith? Read Psalm 139 again.

Hoping

I've been much involved over a number of years with issues related to the Palestinian cause. Many encounters with Jews, Christians and Muslims have had within them the comments: 'It is only *hope* that keeps us going'; 'Without *hope* we have nothing else to cling to.' In the search for Jessica and Holly we kept hopeful. The community wanted the Church to speak for them and a message was declared to the media every day that 'we remain hopeful'. The buttress of that hope was essential to enable the families and the community to face each day.

Praying

Our hope was contained in our prayers. I have become convinced that we don't need fine words in our prayers but we do need to take time to pray. God is quite prepared to listen to a prayer that says, 'I have no words for prayer – please help me.' The community of Soham came to know and experience that for themselves, and people just stopped when they needed to pray and were silent – no words were needed. We also found words and used them, sometimes powerfully, to encapsulate the heartache and anxiety that was being felt. We still need to do that in our lives and witness as each day comes.

Grieving
Walking with faith at the heart of pain became reality for Soham on the 17th August 2002 as the bodies of the children were found. It still feels now like standing on the edge of a bottomless pit, knowing that others had plunged over the edge emotionally. What had been feared and remained unspoken had become real. I felt that ministry was fulfilled by grieving. In grieving we came to see how the working out of grief was needed. As Christ's people we shared the grief of family and community and, as a tidal wave of emotion covered Soham, Christians sought comfort for themselves and for others, keeping our Candles of Hope burning; now they had become Candles of Love.

Loving
The capacity you have for loving is actually far bigger than you ever thought possible . . . believe me. The more that love was expressed to all who came the more love we discovered we had. That continues now in the daily working out of ministry that is not confined to Soham. Love is not conquered by death; love will, and always does, win through. One Candle of Love can illuminate a whole room of darkness and hate.

Caring
Through our Soham sharing I have seen more clearly, in practical ministry with people in all kinds of situations, that loving needs practical outworking. The care that we offer at the same time as we love is vital. It is the way in which another person feels that we are sharing the love

of God in Christ with them. Caring provides the backbone of our loving – it enables what is felt to be tangible and to be expressed in reality.

Listening
The Church often feels that it needs to speak – it has a longing to tell. Yet in praying, words were sometimes not needed. In Soham we drew on the experience of the Samaritans to share with us the listening and caring role. Volunteers worked long hours as the visitor numbers grew and grew. As a result, I feel that I have become more aware in daily ministry of the need to listen, really listen. We should try to catch even what is not being said but what may be felt. We can listen to the heart and soul of another. And we can listen more to God instead of spending most of our devotional time in telling him how things are.

Forgiving
I have struggled through these long months facing issues of forgiveness and mercy, the grace and compassion that God will show to all who ask for it. In an early interview on the day the children's bodies were discovered I was asked the question 'People may well feel angry – what have you to say about anger?' It was a live interview for a foreign satellite station, and I immediately replied, 'I'm so angry now – and I want to stay in my anger, but I know that to do so for long will plunge me into the same darkness that has killed the children.' The need to forgive is hard to accept. But as a gospel imperative we have to declare it. A keynote verse for all situations is 'Do not be overcome by evil, but overcome evil with good' (Romans 12:21, NIV).

Richard Holloway in *On Forgiveness* writes, 'It makes no sense to command people to forgive, and there are clearly situations where every instinct of justice commands us not to forgive. Nevertheless, when true forgiveness happens it is one of the most astonishing and liberating of the human experiences . . . The real beauty and power of forgiveness is that it can deliver the future to us.'[1]

In difficult and stressful work I hung on to faith. I needed to do so or it felt as though darkness would tear it from me. In Ely Cathedral we sang a hymn which held all our experiences together.

Lord, the light of Your love is shining,
in the midst of the darkness, shining:
Jesus, Light of the world, shine upon us;
set us free by the truth You now bring us –
shine on me, shine on me.[2]

Graham Kendrick

May that same light shine in the darkness for you and, discovering 'faith at the heart of pain', may you firmly walk the Way of Jesus.

1   Richard Holloway, *On Forgiveness*, Canongate, 2002, p.12-13.

2   Graham Kendrick © Make Way Music, P.O. Box 263, Croydon CR9 5AP. Used by permission.

Christ has
No body now on earth but yours;
No hands but yours;
No feet but yours;
Yours are the eyes
Through which is to look out
Christ's compassion to the world;
Yours are the feet
With which he is to go about
Doing good;
Yours are the hands
With which he is to bless now.

attributed to St. Teresa of Avila

*Set before our minds and hearts, O heavenly Father, the
example of our Lord Jesus Christ, who, when he was upon
earth, found his refreshment in doing the will of him that sent
him, and in finishing his work. When many are coming and
going, and there is little leisure, give us grace to remember him
who knew neither impatience of spirit nor confusion of work,
but in the midst of all his labours held communion with thee,
and even upon earth was still in heaven; where now he reigns
with thee and the Holy Spirit; world without end. Amen.*

Dean Vaughan

I was busy in the little kitchen of our holiday cottage in Yorkshire. I was very hot and bothered, hurrying to get a meal ready on time. Suddenly a voice seemed to whisper: Listen to the song God is singing for you. I did so, and immediately I heard the music of the little babbling stream which trickled over the stones through the garden.

How often in the rush of life it is necessary to stop what one is doing; to open one's whole self to listen to what God is saying. His song refreshes, restores and steadies the heart and mind.

Jean Coggan

Every now and then go away, have a little relaxation. For when you come back to your work, your judgement will be surer, since to remain constantly at work, you lose your power of judgement. Go some distance away because then the work appears smaller, and more of it can be taken in at a glance, and a lack of harmony or proportion is more readily seen.

Leonardo da Vinci

[In times of tiredness and stress] I turn to the Bible, to David's Psalms, and discover a principle that when emotionally shell-shocked by the battles of life, I should vent my frustration and anger on God. There are some who say: 'Oh no! We must never be angry with God.' For David, described as a man after God's own heart, and for me, there was and is no other way. I did not ask to be born. I did not ask to be a hospice doctor. I cannot cope with so much negativity. *Damn it, God, I cannot cope!* There is so much suffering, so much apparent unfairness. . . . Being angry with God is a necessity for me. Without this avenue of release, I could not continue as a hospice physician . . . The Psalms I find most helpful are those that express weariness of spirit as well as more obvious anger. It is not just the former I identify with: I need to be angry too. And to thank God that, in his infinite capacity to love and to give, he is able to absorb all my anger – and more.

Robert G. Twycross

God give thee
Time for the task
Wisdom for the work,
Grace for the way,
Love to the last.

Anonymous

My Ten Commandments

Thou shalt not worry, for worry is the most unproductive of all human activities.

Thou shalt not be fearful, for most of the things we fear never come to pass.

Thou shalt not cross bridges before you get to them, for no one yet has succeeded in accomplishing this.

Thou shalt face each problem as it comes. You can handle only one at a time anyway.

Thou shalt not take problems to bed with you for they make very poor bedfellows.

Thou shalt not borrow other people's problems. They can take better care of them than you can.

Thou shalt not try to relive yesterday for good or ill – it is gone. Concentrate on what is happening in your life today.

Thou shalt count thy blessings, never overlooking the small ones, for a lot of small blessings add up to a big one.

Thou shalt be a good listener, for only when you listen do you hear ideas different from your own. It's very hard to learn something new when you're talking.

Thou shalt not become bogged down by frustration, for 90 per cent of it is rooted in self-pity and it will only interfere with positive action.

Elodie Armstrong

Scientific research, like any other kind of worthwhile activity, is full of boring routine and frustrating blind alleys. Theoretical physicists generate a lot of crumpled pieces of paper as what seemed like good ideas fail to work out quite right. The payoff for all this weary activity is the sense of wonder as, once in a while, some new aspect of the physical world becomes understood by us . . . When scientists enjoy the sense of wonder in this way, whether they know it or not, they are praising God for the magnificence of his creation.

John Polkinghorne

How completely satisfying to turn from our limitations to a God who has none. Eternal years lie in his heart. For him time does not pass, it remains; and those who are in Christ share with him all the riches of limitless time and endless years. God never hurries. There are no deadlines against which he must work. Only to know this is to quiet our spirits and relax our nerves.

A. W. Tozer

Principles

Christine Kinch

When I was at high school, which seems like a million years ago, I came top of the class in dietetics and bottom in cookery. In other words I knew the theory but found the practical a bit harder. It was a good hint that my cookery was never to improve, and of a dual Christian life ahead as a minister's wife and local journalist. It is an interesting combination of lives, which has produced many a 'talk', but where, of course, all the best stories are, and will have to remain forever, off the record.

Having a strong Christian faith has given many people a rock to hold on to during stormy days, but I have found it can also throw you up against the breakers in the most unexpected ways. And the briefest read of the New Testament or Church history shows I am not alone. So many fascinating and challenging things have happened as I have walked the precipice between my two lives, but one stands out particularly.

I found myself in the front row at a school play, seated among the VIPs. When your own children are 'performing' there are good reasons to attend such events. And we missed none of our own offsprings' attempts at stardom. It is harder, however, to feel enthused when it takes up the only free night that week and you know no one on stage. And I had no idea as I took my seat that what should have been a very happy event would turn out to have such consequences . . .

I had only gone because no one else in the office wanted to, and the school told me a character based on me (based on ME!) was in the play – a rip-roaring musical. Yes, it was amusing to watch someone dressed as an 'ace reporter' staggering around on very high heels and writing constantly in a notebook. I made a mental note to wear sensible shoes from now on. The whole evening should have been wonderful – but it wasn't, even though the scenery, the lights, the music, the costumes were all fantastic, and the children in the church school had all learned their lines perfectly and their diction was superb.

The story of the play was that a school had to close because of financial difficulties, and the head teacher decided to go into outer space to bring back some moon treasure to save the day. There were three stages mounted on blocks, one for the head's office, one for outer space and the third for the school choir. The play proceeded beautifully until the 'head' got into outer space where he underwent a series of hilariously funny adventures, the last of which was to be gobbled up by a black hole.

Down through the audience came a young white lad, suitably blacked up, with dreadlocks and a huge cloak. He danced round the 'head' singing, 'I'm a great big Black Hole.' Although he was young, his voice was very good and he sounded for all the world like one of the many Rastafarians we have in the city. Eventually he enveloped his prey in his cloak. The young actor then slipped down, under the stage, and out from the Black Hole's cloak fell a tin of corned beef.

We all roared with laughter and the play proceeded with the rest of the cast wondering how to save their head from oblivion. And then, a dainty blonde girl, dressed all in white, came down the aisle singing, 'I'm a tiny little White Hole.' She zapped the Black Hole with her wand, until he lay stone dead. He took ages to die and got much applause for his spoofing. The 'head' then came back to life, returned to earth with his moon treasure, and the school was saved.

I didn't realise the end had come. I waited in vain to learn, along with the children, that for black and white to work together in harmony was the real treasure that had been discovered. But no. That was it – white had once again triumphed over black. I turned to the deputy head and said: 'It's a good job there are no black families here.'

'Oh, we don't think about that sort of thing,' she said. I stood up, glared at her and walked out, making sure I reached the car park before bursting into tears of rage. I felt too choked to speak to anyone. Did Christ in the Temple feel like this? In a place of goodness and light there lurked something utterly wrong. I went on to the Tuesday Fellowship in the centre of Wolverhampton, the place where many of these children would one day work, alongside people from all races and cultures. A wonderful, vibrant, welcoming place. My husband was leading a discussion on slavery in the Old Testament and of John Wesley's work against it in his own lifetime. The black members told their own tales of feeling unwelcome when they first arrived in Britain.

I sobbed out my incoherent story and they hugged me and said that it really didn't matter and that I would feel better in the morning. But I didn't feel better because I had no right to feel better. I couldn't forgive such blatant racism. So I told my editor the whole sorry tale and he suggested I ring the school head and talk to him. The head slammed the phone down on me, so I used that which is said to be mightier than the sword – my pen. I wrote to him and then wrote a piece in my weekly column, being careful to name neither the school nor anyone involved.

Within the following week I received a carrier bag full of hate mail. Parents rang me. Villagers rang me. Children rang me. The racism, they told me, was all in my mind. And I was an idiot if I didn't know what a black hole in space was. Then a young boy summed it all up: 'What you don't realise,' he told me, 'is that black *is* bad and white *is* good.'

Those where his exact words.

Trying to hold on to a set of Christian principles in a situation like this and taking on a whole church school was not easy, especially as it *was* a church school, but I am only a Methodist because I believe so passionately in the universality of the gospel, which has to equate with the equality of all people. I knew I must stand firm.

Firm until a week later, when I had to go to report on a Parish Council meeting in that same village.

I waited until the last moment before arriving and, at the end, was attempting to make my hasty exit when a woman who had been shouting angrily at her neighbour turned to me and said: 'And as for you . . .'. I waited to be vilified again, but she went on, 'Why does your paper refuse to print details of our jumble sale each year? I've been trying for three years to get a look-in, but to no avail!' I sent up a wee thank you. A quick glance at the ceiling is all God gets at times of stress but he has a great sense of humour. Life was starting to get back to normal.

What a flat-footed attempt I made to do the right thing. What a coward I was in the way I confronted the situation. I still don't know what the right thing would have been, but I am sure I messed it up. I would love to think that my outburst caused an entire village to discuss a subject that had never before crossed its corporate mind, but I know this is very unlikely.

So, again, it's top marks for theory, but bottom for practice. It was ever thus!

Lord, you have come
to offer us
abundant life
rich
overflowing
energetic
and exciting.
When our lives are tired
and our spirits stagnate
come to us with your resources
of humour and hope
lest
in lukewarm sadness
we forget your power.
When we become
cotton-wool Christians
softened by age or wealth,
grasp us with the urgency of your gospel
lest
in feeble cowardice
we deny your resurrection.
When our gifts remain unoffered
and our talents unused
expose our light
to the darkness of the world
lest
in needless fear
we flicker and die.
Lord, we offer back to you
abundant life
rich
overflowing
energetic
and exciting.

David Jenkins

> *It is character, not time, we*
> *want to do our work.*
>
> Marcus Dods

Discouraged in the work of life,
Disheartened by its load,
Shamed by its failures or its fears,
I sink beside the road;
But let me only think of thee
And then new hope springs up in me.

Samuel Longfellow

Everything that they [the Celtic Christians] touched, every tool that they handled, was done with respect and reverence; every activity performed with a sense of the presence of God, indeed done in partnership with him. So life was lived at two levels. Each successive task was performed seriously, carefully, with attention, and simultaneously becoming the occasion for finding the presence of God, and in particular the three members of the Trinity, since much of the work was routine and it could, therefore, be done rhythmically in the name of Father, Son and Holy Spirit.

Esther de Waal

Our powers become rapidly exhausted in our work. If we occupy ourselves exclusively with the world, even for the purpose of serving it, we become superficial, unreal and ineffective.

J. H. Oldham

In all our attempts to pray, our changing culture is working against us. All our time-saving machines, from cars to aeroplanes, to telephones and emails have us going ever faster instead of more leisurely. Everyone seems to be running out of time for everything, and prayer is in danger of being left out even when we need it most.

Avery Brooke

The day returns and brings us the petty round of irritating concerns and duties. Help us . . . to perform them with laughter and kind faces. Let cheerfulness abound with industry. Give us to go blithely on our business all this day, bring us to our resting beds weary and content and undishonoured, and grant us in the end the gift of sleep.

Robert Louis Stevenson

Under a spreading chestnut tree
The village smithy stands;
The smith, a mighty man is he,
With large and sinewy hands;
And the muscles of his brawny arms
Are strong as iron bands.

His hair is crisp, and black, and long,
His face is like the tan;
His brow is wet with sweat,
He earns what'er he can,
And looks the whole world in the face,
For he owes not any man.

Week in, week out, from morn till night,
You can hear his bellows blow;
You can hear him swing his heavy sledge,
With measured beat and slow,
Like a sexton ringing the village bell,
When the evening sun is low.

Toiling – rejoicing – sorrowing,
Onward through life he goes;
Each morning sees some task begin,
Each evening sees its close;
Something attempted, something done,
Has earned a night's repose.

H. W. Longfellow

Haven't you noticed how a smith, mason, or carpenter, or any other craftsman, however much his back is against the wall, will never sell or pawn the tools of his trade? If he did, how could he earn his living? That is how we should think of the Bible: just as mallets, hammers, saws, chisels, axes and hatchets are the tools of the craftsman's trade, so the books of the prophets and the apostles, and all Scripture inspired by the Holy Spirit, are the tools of our salvation.

John Chrysostom

A potter at the wheel is totally involved with his pot until it is finished. You feel the rhythm, you scarcely dare to admit it in case you break the flow; you just hang on by your eyebrows letting it flow through your hands.

Bernard Leach

May there be nothing in this day's work of which we shall be ashamed when the sun has set, nor in the eventide of our life when our task is done, and we go to our home to meet thy face.

Walter Rauschenbusch

God is my Help

Brenda Thornton

I'm one of those people who has happy memories of school and Sunday school. I enjoyed being surrounded by friends and caring adults, who made my early years both stimulating and comfortable. 'Boring' was not part of my vocabulary; there was never time to be bored. Life was enjoyable. Christians weren't killjoys, but people who knew how to mix routine and chores with laughter and fun. Partly because of this background and because of my personal inclinations, I knew that I wanted to be a teacher when I grew up.

Experiences as a young teenager, in church and in other activities, confirmed my intention to teach and gave me a goal to work towards. Vocation and service are two words that played an important role in my life from then on, and they still do. At home we were encouraged, by our parents, to follow a simple prayer which began 'God is my help in every need.' We used this prayer not only in times of difficulty, but as a constant reminder of God's involvement in all aspects of our life. This prayer still remains important to me over half a century later.

School – exams – college – more exams and school again, but this time as a teacher. Now the challenges began. I wanted, intended to be a 'good' teacher with time for individuals as well as groups. 'Teach' has a variety of definitions: instruct, train, enable, explain, are just a few. I always aimed to involve all these elements in my work, with differing degrees of success.

Starting my career in a secondary school in a 'challenging' part of Huddersfield, the West Riding mill town that was my home, I quickly became absorbed into its whole life. One after-school club was for the final year students – at that time year 4 (in current educational terminology year 10) where the emphasis was on social skills. Games, dancing and refreshments were the main elements, with the emphasis on 'how to behave' in a variety of situations. They were fun times with a very positive outcome. Students learnt an important lesson: that teachers are human too, and that they, the students, could also teach, particularly in the area of dance! Like many teachers who are Christians, I continued to be an involved participant in the local church, where I was 'fed and encouraged', enabling me to teach by example and not just instruction.

Marriage involved a new job in a new place, the beautiful city of York. There we quickly became involved and included in the church and I settled into a new school. York was, and still is, a city where cycling is a major mode of transport. As the PE teacher I took teams to various places for matches and athletic events. Coming from the foothills of the Pennines I had very little previous experience of being on a bike, which soon became evident to my students. It didn't take long for one of the brave ones to suggest that 'Miss' went on the inside of the convoy and that she would look after me – just another delightful example of the teacher becoming the student and the student becoming the teacher.

A new stage of life's journey began with the birth of our first son, followed by another move. This time it was not just across England's largest county, but across the ocean, to hot, steamy West Africa. My husband Brian had been appointed to the Church Missionary Society Bookshop in Sierra Leone. I had no intention of being anything other than an indulgent mum to our infant son, but the call to teach was too strong and I found myself at the Annie Walsh Grammar School for Girls in Freetown. How different it was. Some students were still in school in their early twenties, but how keen they were to learn, and a real joy to teach. It gave me another opportunity to live out my faith in the work situation. Indeed, I have seen this as a great privilege throughout my career, aware of just how fortunate I am.

Back in England, and after the arrival of our second son, we moved from the north of England to North London. I had changed direction in my teaching career prior to coming to London, and now I was focusing on remedial/special needs work. Joys and cares are an essential part of teaching, but they are much more acute in this field. In my experience so many youngsters who have difficulty in acquiring basic skills also have low self-esteem, particularly when they get beyond the age of 10. I saw my work as multifaceted, as I tried to address all aspects of students' needs. I have been rewarded with times of joy when pupils have met with success in various aspects of personal development, and have also had times of great frustration, when nothing seems to work or go right.

Each child is, I believe, 'a child of God', and it was important for me to remember this and to put it into practice. A large, multiracial, multicultural comprehensive school, situated in a very mixed area of the London Borough of Enfield, brought me many tensions at times but great benefits, too. To see pupils working together and helping each other regardless of colour, gender or religious background is always uplifting. Conversely, having to watch division and mistrust, for whatever reason, is a real challenge.

Youngsters often arrive in school with 'baggage', the kind of load with which one cannot identify. Varying cultural practices do not always sit easily together and at times it is difficult to remain calm, patient and professional whilst trying to help. It was in this type of situation where a period of reflection and quiet prayer often helped me to continue the work. I found that child protection issues could be distressing in the extreme. This sometimes arose due to adults' varying attitudes towards children as individuals, and towards children's place in society.

As far as working life is concerned my final move came as a result of relocation. It coincided with a move in education towards inclusion, which meant that more children with special needs were being educated in mainstream schools alongside peer-group students. It gave me the opportunity to put into practice what I had learnt whilst doing the DIPSEN course at London University. Children with statements of educational

111

need covering learning difficulties, visual and hearing impairment, Downs syndrome and autism were joined, in my final years in teaching, by those with behavioural difficulties. Each needed individual programmes to work alongside mainstream provision.

It was good to teach in a smaller school but initially I missed the previous rich multiethnic and cultural diversity. The principal of the school was a practising Christian who believed that every child was special and important. I was asked to become the Child Protection Co-ordinator in the school, and after much prayer and reflection agreed to undertake this demanding role. In this area it was important, for me, to base my working life on my own faith practices, where daily devotions and corporate worship gave perspective. I certainly needed to remember 'who I was and where I came from', when this particular aspect of my duties was called upon. To be totally non-judgemental and professional was the way I could be of help. Being a listening ear for the students was both a privilege and an enormous challenge. I reflected often that if I had had all the negative life experiences of many of my students, just how would I have coped?

Now retired, I am glad that I was able to teach for so many years and I thank God for all I have learned from my colleagues and my students.

I will try to give them all that the years have brought to my own soul. God help me to give what he gave, myself, and to make that self worth something to somebody. Teach me to love all, as he has loved, for the sake of the possibilities locked up in every soul.

Alice Freeman Palmer, speaking of teaching

I dreaded Monday morning; but the reality was worse than I could ever have imagined. A class of forty or so – they seemed to be all the children in the world – forty or so nicely behaved little girls and boys fastened their bright eyes on me as Mr Boxhall introduced me to my classroom. With the uncanny instinct of ten-year-olds they realised that I was delivered into their hands; that I was not a disciplinarian; that I was as uncertain of myself and my surroundings as a Jenny Wren. In calling the register I mispronounced a name. All the children shouted with laughter.

Anne Treneer

You know, O Lord, the duties that lie before us this day, and the sins that so easily beset us. Guide us, strengthen us, and protect us, O Lord, our strength and our Redeemer.

Mabel Dearmer

113

A 'second journey', is when you come to the end of one phase in your life and you go through a period of great darkness, where all the milestones, all the markers shift. And then it all clarifies and gels, and off you go again.

When you get to these crossroads, you either go sideways and try something quite new, or you go on, on the same path but in a completely different way. As I have said, when I got to my own personal crossroads, I wondered whether to go sideways and teach theology, or whether to go on writing, though writing very different kinds of books – which is what I did. That was my second journey. My first journey was behind me, and I didn't want to cling to it.

Susan Howatch

I've been lucky. I had a vision, which I felt was given, and I was able to do something practical about it. It was a day by day business, but there was a vision – which I had to follow after in the most practical, definite, raising-money, learning, interesting-other-people way possible!

Cicely Saunders

Each day, each week, each month, each year, is a new chance given you by God. A new chance, a new leaf, a new life – this is the golden, the unspeakable gift which each day offers you.

F. W. Farrar

I can picture one teacher there – I can't recall her name. She was short and spare, and I remember her eager jutting chin. Quite unexpectedly one day (in the middle, I think, of an arithmetic lesson) she suddenly launched forth on a speech on life and religion. 'All of you,' she said, 'every *one* of you will pass through a time when you will face despair. If you never face despair, you will never have faced, or become a Christian, or known a Christian life. To be a Christian you must face and accept the life that Christ faced and lived; you must enjoy things as he enjoyed things; be as happy as he was at the marriage at Cana, know the peace and happiness that it means to be in harmony with God and with God's will. But you must also know, as he did, what it means to be alone in the Garden of Gethsemane, to feel that all your friends have forsaken you, and that God *himself* has forsaken you. Hold on then to the belief that it is *not* the end. If you love, you will suffer, and if you do not love, you do not know the meaning of a Christian life.'

She then returned to the problems of compound interest with her usual vigour, but it is odd that those few words, more than any sermon I have ever heard, remained with me, and years later they were to come back to me and give me hope at a time when despair had me in its grip. She was a dynamic figure and also, I think, a *fine* teacher; I wish I could have been taught by her longer.

Agatha Christie

I know how much you grieve over those who are under your care: those you try to help and fail, those you cannot help. Have faith in God and remember that he will in his own way and in his own time complete what we so poorly attempt. Often we do not achieve for others the good we intend; but we achieve something, something that goes on from our effort. Good is an overflow. Where we generously and sincerely intend it, we are engaged in a work of creation which may be mysterious even to ourselves ... God can always show us, if we will a higher and better way; and we can only learn to love by loving. Remember that all our failures are ultimately failures in love. Imperfect love must not be condemned and rejected, but made perfect.

Iris Murdoch

Remember, other people's estimate of your work cannot change its quality. Pronouncing good work bad does not make it bad; nor does calling bad work good make it good; nor have reports on paper, favourable or unfavourable, power to add or take away one iota of accomplished good. The first question for you, about all your work, must be: Is it good in God's sight? In other words, whether my talents were two or fifty, did I do my best?

Catherine Bramwell-Booth

And give me, good Lord, an humble, lowly, quiet, peaceable, patient, charitable, kind and filial and tender mind, every shade, in fact, of charity, with all my words and all my works and all thoughts, to have a taste of thy holy blessed Spirit.

St. Thomas More

A man who was in charge of building a great cathedral was pestered by an apprentice who wanted to design and arrange the glass for just one of the windows. Although he did not want to discourage so laudable an ambition, neither did the boss want to risk the waste of costly material. Finally he told the apprentice that he could try his hand on one small window, but that he would have to provide the material for it himself.

Undaunted, the apprentice gathered up all the bits of glass that had been cut off and discarded, and with these scraps he worked out a design of rare beauty. When the cathedral was opened to the public, people stood in awe and praise before the one small window designed by the apprentice.

Everyone can put to good use their own little bits of time, talent, influence, ambition, energy, and weave them into lives of beauty and goodness and rare value.

Author unknown

Sharing the Load

Graham Leighton

For most of my working life I have driven articulated
lorries. I also have a PSV Double Decker Licence. When
I was asked to write an article on what it was like to take
God to work with me, I really had to think, because,
without being blasé about it, I knew that whatever
situation I was in I would ask God for help, and he
would always be there to answer my prayer, sometimes
in remarkable ways. So I have tried to remember the
various times when I especially knew that he has been
with me.

Once, as a coach driver I had been with a coach firm for a
few months and was taking out elderly folk from a
retirement home. I had 53 passengers on my coach,
which had a lift on the back. It made it very hard and
demanding work. You either love this kind of work or
hate it. I loved it and was able to witness one-to-one or
even to four or five passengers at a time. This particular
day I had been to Weston-Super-Mare (for the umpteenth
time) – the coach knew how to get there without me, if it
had been possible. Anyway, I had had some Christian
choruses on the tape and the people seemed to like them.
One or two had moaned a little at first, but had shut up.

The trip home was very good. After I got home I thanked the Lord and asked if he would put the Holy Spirit over the whole coach.

Two days later I picked up another crowd from a newly built home. As they were boarding a couple came over to me and said, 'You are a Christian, aren't you?' Somewhat surprised I replied that I was and we chatted. They asked me if I had any choruses and I told them I had and would play them when we got moving. Once again we were going to Weston-Super-Mare.

While I was talking to them, I felt really peaceful. I had never felt like this before. In truck and coach driving we tend to be moaned at most of the time. This particular summer had been hot and sunny, and as we drove back home I looked in my interior mirror at the passengers and everyone looked so very happy and peaceful it could only be the work of the Holy Spirit. We came back that day 'like a rocket sled on rails'. I have never had a drive back from Weston like it; I felt as though we travelled the two and a half hours in ten minutes, and as the people got off, they all thanked me.

As a truck driver, without sounding condescending, you tend to meet the more verbal type of people. I remember some years ago, trucking to Heathrow, making deliveries to companies around the airport. I pulled in at my first call one particular night. The truck was so full, with more volume than weight, that I'd fastened the straps so tightly with the security cord that I couldn't free them. I needed a screwdriver or something sharp to tease them open. I asked one of the bald-headed stack-a truck drivers if he had one. He said, 'No, but I've got something sharp enough to do it.' After a few minutes he came over and stood about one inch away from me in the lorry, put his hand inside his jacket and pulled out a bayonet (that would fix on the end of a rifle). I was surprised, but you do get used to these things. He said to me with a grin, 'Is this sharp enough?' 'Yes, thank you,' I returned. Having worked in this sort of environment for a good number of years, there are some things that do concern you and this could have been one of them, especially as it was a time of a lot of knife attacks around London. At that precise moment I thanked the Lord that I was his child!

On another occasion I had been away in Scotland two or three nights. I started to run down the east coast on the A1 but I ran out of time in Dunbar. I pulled on to the car park. It seemed desolate, and for some unknown reason I felt agitated for the safety of my vehicle. It wasn't a sleeper cab, so I got the cab ready and pulled the curtains around. While I was doing all this I said to God, 'I don't know why I feel like this, but I do feel so vulnerable and alone. Would you send someone to park beside me even if it's only one vehicle?' Partly believing in faith that it would happen; partly a victim of my own thoughts, *not* believing it would happen, I closed the curtains even though it was still light, and resigned myself to sitting there all evening on my own.

Much to my amazement a matter of five or 10 minutes had gone by when I heard the rumble of a truck. I looked out of the window and saw a truck pull round me to the side. I heard his brakes go on and saw him pull his curtains round. I was surprised by the speed (so to speak) with which the Lord had answered my prayer.

Sometimes when I was away overnight I used to say, 'Lord, I have no food and I don't know the area.' The trucks had no sleeper cabs in those days and the good old lorry driver cafés were closing down due to the building of motorway services. Nearly every time I would reach a café on my way just as my hours were running out on the tachograph. God said he will 'satisfy every need of yours' (Philippians 4:19). Believe me, with a job like trucking you eat as if food can't be grown fast enough! Whenever I take food I always thank God for it (wherever I am) and ask God to bless those who have prepared it.

I also found that when I needed to unload in the days when the load wasn't palletised it was very demanding physically, and most times I ended up hand-balling it myself. I know God not only helped me, but gave me the strength to keep going all day and stay alert to drive. They were very long days.

God has brought me a long way from when I was first saved 26 years ago and I have always had the desire to witness to other drivers. I really believe that he has placed me as Chairman of the CIRT (Christians in Road Transport) to tell truck drivers and anyone working in transport that CIRT is dedicated to the spreading of the gospel. Didn't Jesus say, 'Go into all the world'? I have been in heavy transport for 39 years and I know how much we need Jesus every day of our lives.

As I remember these times and put them down on paper I also remember how hard and tedious this job can be, both mentally and physically. I know that although I am physically strong, I look back and know that if I had not been able to call on the Name of Jesus then all the physical and mental strength would have been to no avail. So I knew he put a backbone of steel in me, and he has also honoured me by my being asked to be the Chairman of this Christian organisation. I have experienced this difficult job myself and can now help other drivers who need to know Jesus for themselves.

I believe that, even though I was quite experienced as an HGV driver when I gave my life to the Lord, I know that my talent for driving is God-given. I believe that God ordained what we are to be before we are born, and that my job as a driver is what he wanted me to do.

I have been blessed, too, in my family life – I have been married for 38 years. Marriage and family life is far from easy in my kind of work, and my wife and my son have often been lonely when I have been away for a week or weeks at a time. But God has helped me in this too, and now we are making up some of the precious time we have lost.

So I thank God for his faithfulness to me – and to him be the praise and the glory.

Throughout the course of your daily life make use of the opportunities offered you to take a new hold on yourself and to welcome God into your life: while you're waiting for the bus, or for your motor to warm up, or for your supper to cook, or for the milk to boil, or for your coffee to cool off, or for a free telephone booth, or for the traffic lights to change . . . don't kill time; no matter how short it is, it can be a moment of grace. The Lord is there, and he invites you to reflection and decision so that you can become a human being in the fullest sense.

Michel Quoist

[Jesus] worked as a carpenter until he was thirty years of age, and during his three-year ministry he worked hard. Even on his holidays he helped people and healed the sick. For that reason some people came to Jesus and asked, 'Don't you rest even on a rest day?' 'No, God always works; if God rested, the world would fall; therefore, while God works, I work also.' According to Christ, therefore, daily living was religion.

Toyohiko Kagawa

God imparteth by the way
Strength sufficient for the day.

J. E. Saxby

Experience counts for something, Lord . . . we have learned a lot over the years. We have met interesting people, we know better how to handle situations; we know ourselves better. Ideas still come to us, we have much to pass on.

Give us new opportunities, Lord, we pray. Use our talents and gifts, perhaps in new ways. May new doors open for us and may we take up new challenges with joy and keenness. May we be easy and cheerful to work with.

Joan Clifford

Above all, we must not be discouraged by difficulties, but must remind ourselves that the more difficult a work is, the slower and more unrewarding it is, the more necessary it is to set to work with great dispatch and make great efforts.

Charles de Foucauld

Try to forget yourself in the service of others. For when we think too much of ourselves and our own interests, we easily become despondent. But when we work with others, our efforts return to bless us.

Sidney Powell

Brother 'A' was bulldozing the top irrigation ditch and found a large hole that couldn't be filled. So this morning I helped install a large metal pipe. My task this afternoon was to dig out the water entrance on both sides of the pipe, and place rock to keep the earth being eaten away. So at 2.30 I took the pickup, filled with rock, over pastures, through three gates, and finally up a very steep and scary 'road' to the top. And there, utterly alone, snow hills all around, an eagle soared and finally perched on an evergreen beside me. I shoved and shaped the ground. In the warm sun I was ecstatic – swept by the wind – creating, with and for water. Epiphany. And I ate an orange!

W. Paul Jones

You must do as well as ever you can whatever God gives you to do; that is the best possible preparation for what he may want you to do next.

Thomas Chalmers

Be diligent. Never be unemployed. Never be triflingly employed. Never *while* away time, nor spend more time at any place than is strictly necessary . . . You have nothing to do but to save souls. Therefore spend and be spent in this work. And go always, not only to those who want you, but to those who want you most.

John Wesley

Wesley ascribed his good health and serenity to early rising (helped by an alarm which 'went off with a thundering noise') and to early prayer, followed by the usual preaching at 5 a.m. He loved regular exercise, even in old age; he had a level temperament and 'though I am always in haste,' he had written when still in his seventies, 'I am never in a hurry; because I never undertake any more work than I can go through with perfect calmness of spirit.' He was also much alone, travelling in his chaise, and thus had time for reading, reflection and more prayer. By his mid-eighties his friends sometimes felt that he preached and wrote too much, but he would not slacken.

John Pollock

They [the early residents of Foxton, Cambs] did not have to plan; the Reeve did that for them, and most of their problems were solved by simply following routine. They did not have to think. All they had to do was work; start their working life at about the age of six and go on working until they dropped dead from fatigue, illness, hunger or old age, which set in at about the age of forty and did not usually last very long. They may have dreamed of something better; they can have had little hope of ever achieving it.

Rowland Parker

I see them now on a summer's day coming home covered in brick dust, their hands blistered, their throats parched and aching for a glass of water. It was never easy work making bricks, and before the days of mechanisation men had to draw the baked bricks from the kilns by hand. Often the heat was so intense that they had to dip old sacks into tubs of water and then drape sacks over their backs before rushing again into the furnace-like chambers. Even though modern machinery has changed all that, the job is still a hard and dangerous one.

Edward Storey

Sustained by God

Jill Brown

I was feeling rather put out – in fact I was decidedly miffed! I was 17, and in the sixth form at school, at a stage when we all had to decide whether we wanted to go on to university, go straight out to work or what? And encouraged by the biology teacher, I had decided to apply to medical school. That wasn't the problem. At this moment I was at an 'Enquirers' Group', which our church ran for teenagers, and anyone else who might be thinking about baptism and joining the church. I had been brought up in a 'church family' . . . Sunday school and church every Sunday, Bible class in the afternoon, youth group on Saturday nights. On this particular evening the minister had asked us all what we were going to do when we left school. When I said I wanted to be a doctor, (at which point people usually made approving noises!) he just asked why. Being a fairly stroppy teenager I replied, 'Because that's what I want to do.' To which he said very simply, 'That's an awful pity if God wants you to do something else, like being a teacher' – and moved on to whoever was sitting next to me. I thought maybe I wouldn't even bother to come to the group again if that's what it was like . . . But I did, because I wasn't going to let anyone think he had 'got to me'.

Two or three weeks later the minister said something to me that has stayed with me ever since: 'Jesus is as real as if you could see him sitting on the next chair.' And suddenly to me Jesus was as real as that. In fact, as I walked home that night, I wasn't alone – one of those experiences that you store up and treasure, and ponder. I didn't have the words to describe how I felt, or what it meant to me, but I knew then that the stories I had heard of Christ risen and alive today were really true, and that he was someone I wanted to follow.

To my enormous relief, as with excitement I explored my newly-found faith, and tested out whether or not I should continue on the path I thought I had chosen, the doors continued to open, and I completed my medical training. As I cycled the three miles from college to the medical school during my first year, over a clanking manhole cover, round the corner where the early morning smell of freshly-roasted coffee beans drifted across the road, I knew I was 'happy now', deeply content, and thanked God for his goodness to me.

That was all a long while ago, but in many ways those experiences are fresh and close at hand. Throughout the years, that sense of an accompanying God, sometimes closer, sometimes distant, has sustained and enabled me. When I've had to make decisions that seemed difficult at the time, I have relied on an awareness that sometimes we do make choices without knowing the right answer, but that God will work with us, even through our mistakes, as long as we are as honest with him as we possibly can be.

At college, life is coloured by exams, and by the relief of passing them and 'qualifying'. At work, I discovered that, once I was qualified as a doctor, that was when the learning began. I knew nothing! So I had to learn when it was important to make a decision immediately on what I did know, and when it was much better to say, 'I don't know, but I'll find out and come back to you.' I found that when I did make a decision that I wasn't comfortable with, then I was not at peace until I had gone back and done something else about it, checked it out, revised my original thinking, asked advice.

I slowly discovered that life is a continual learning process – whatever path God has for you, you find how much there is to learn and explore, and the sheer excitement of discovery. I learnt the value of teamwork, appreciating the experience of colleagues, recognising the support of other team members, remembering to say thank you, the importance of encouragement.

And as I learnt these things, I recognised, too, how blessed I had been in my home and upbringing, church-based, grounded in the faith of my parents and grandparents, encouraged in my studies, and above all, loved. I discovered how much grief there is in the world, how much pain people carry in their hearts and how this so often affects their physical and emotional well-being. I found out how many people are unloved, need someone to listen to them, have no sense of their own value. And so I began to learn to listen.

Learning to listen, both to other people and to God, is perhaps the hardest task, and years later I find I am still learning. What I have valued enormously over the years are those people who have listened with me, who have prayed with me, friends who have become close in God's presence as we have tried to listen together.

The shock of becoming aware of child abuse as I worked in Accident & Emergency in the early 1960s, is vivid in my memory. Later I worked with children and families in the community, where there was sometimes abuse, often distress and dysfunction, or where delayed development and physical disability brought the family hardship and grief. I do not know how I would have managed without an accompanying God. I learnt that faith does not have to be overt to be valid, that the way people are treated and respected offers them dignity and value whatever the task or interaction.

Frustration and sometimes anger at the way resources are shared, and the unfairness of life for some people has been a challenge, when I have had to try to think through anger against both people and God. How can life be so unfair for some children, for some adults? Why is the world such an unfair place in which to live – some with more than enough for comfort, others without the necessities for survival? That we live in a 'fallen world', where things are not the way God wants them, is a way of dealing with this but there are many questions to which there are no easy answers – and these are metaphorically stacked up on a top shelf to be considered at length at some later date! Some of them slip out of mind; some are reawakened by fresh experience.

Some of the ways in which we think about suffering, whether it is in illness or tragedy, are coloured by our understanding of God, a God who neither desires nor wills suffering. He is a God who will hold both us and our anger, even as we weep and beat him on the chest with our fists like an angry child. What a relief to be allowed to be angry, and to be held until the world is a possible place to be again!

In the same way, our understanding of God influences how we think about healing and cure. People would always like instant cures, but that is not always possible. I am comforted by the knowledge that the words 'health' and 'wholeness' have the same root, and the awareness that people can become 'whole' without 'cure' in the sense that this is generally accepted. I have been blessed by many people who have been 'whole' despite suffering from chronic illness, or even terminal illness, and have clearly been 'walking with God' on their journey. In working with children with disability, I have been amazed by their courage and generous spirits, how they may be more concerned about another's progress than about wanting to win a game for themselves, and humbled by the courage and patience of their parents.

Reflecting on what has sustained me, day in and day out, takes me back again to those early days when I became a follower in the way. Firstly, the Bible words that my father gave me when I was baptised: 'I will be with you wherever you go. I will direct your path.' And secondly, something from a book I was given, *A Diary of Private Prayer* by John Baillie. In it there is a prayer for each day of the month, and a space to write. One of the passages chosen for the day is part of Tennyson's poem, *Idylls of the King,* which says, 'More things are wrought by prayer than this world dreams of . . .' Wow! What a statement – and despite our disbelief and even surprise when prayers are answered, what a vision this poet had. And I become again acutely aware that I am sustained, not by anything I can do or have done, but by the grace of God, a God who continually picks me up, dusts me down, and lets me start again.

*They who tread the path of labour follow where
my feet have trod;
They who work without complaining do the holy
will of God;
Nevermore thou needest seek Me; I am with thee
ev'rywhere;
Raise the stone, and thou shalt find Me; cleave the
wood and I am there.*

*Where the many toil together, there am I among
My own;
Where the tired workman sleepeth, there am I
with him alone.
I, the Peace which passeth knowledge, dwell amid
the daily strife,
I, the Bread of heaven, am broken in the sacrament
of life.*

*Every task, however simple, sets the soul that does
it free;
Every deed of love and mercy done to man, is done
to Me.
Nevermore thou needest seek Me; I am with thee
ev'rywhere;
Raise the stone, and thou shalt find Me; cleave the
wood and I am there.*

Henry van Dyke

134

To serve right gloriously . . .

Don't just sit on the sidelines!

Gary Streeter

'Hear anything?' Janet, my wife asked tentatively upon my return. After a frustrating year of asking God to clarify his will for my life, I had decided to take a day off from my busy life as a partner in a large law firm to try and spend it in prayer and fasting.

'Yes,' I replied, 'I believe God is calling us into politics.' It was the first time politics had ever been mentioned in our charismatic house-church home. Her reply was instant. 'Oh no!' she gasped, and she was right! It was December 1985, I was 30 years of age, a successful corporate lawyer, knowing next to nothing about politics (like most Christians in those days), but we did not dare ignore the call of God on my life to step into the political arena. Doors flew open, rapid progress followed, and I was elected to Plymouth City Council just six months later. My political education began in earnest, largely through mistakes, as I shinned my way up and down a steep learning curve. Six years later I was elected to Westminster and have been there ever since, two years a minister under John Major, three years in the shadow Cabinet, many campaigns and projects tucked under my belt, trying to work out that calling as best I can.

'Does your faith help in your line of work?' some people ask. 'Wrong question,' I reply. The issue is not, does it help, but is it true? Does God exist, is the Bible true, did Jesus live and die and rise from the dead? Did God call me into politics? If yes, get on with it. Work it out in practice. That's what my wife and I, supported by our two wonderful children, are trying to do.

For years Christians have turned their backs on the political arena, leaving key decisions about healthcare, education and family support to others. Why? Of course it is tough and there are compromises to be made – just like any other sphere of work. But why would we who have a true picture of human nature, we who should have compassion for the poorest in our midst, we who have access to heavenly wisdom to tackle some of society's greatest problems, why would we willingly abdicate our responsibilities, just because it is a tough, unforgiving place to serve? During my 10 years in Parliament by far the most biting criticism I have received has come from Christians. Why won't you follow our agenda? How can you be a Conservative? Why did you vote that way and not this? We still have so much to learn about seeking to serve our nation by working together finding unity and purpose in diversity. But things are slowly changing. In the early years many would ask: how can you be a politician and a Christian? Few ask that today. I believe that God is doing a new thing in our midst, making it clear that he wants his people to be involved in every sector of society, being salt and light wherever they are called to be. Including politics.

Since November 1997 I have met at least fortnightly with other MPs, one fellow Conservative, two Labour, one Liberal Democrat and one Ulster Unionist, to pray for and encourage each other. It has become a place of security and real encouragement as relationships have gone deep, carefully and slowly built. Several times a year we meet with our spouses and children to widen the circle and strengthen our friendships. We seek to reach out to other MPs who profess a faith, although in extremely hectic lives we constantly fall short of our aspirations. There are good people who stand alongside us and the team is growing. Even though there has been Christian witness here for generations we sense that there is a new season of the work here at Westminster just beginning.

But fellowship alone, though vital, is not enough. We want to have an effect on the laws and leadership which Parliament provides. There are many policy differences between us and we constantly vote in different lobbies, as is natural and proper. There is no single Christian policy on VAT or transport, or even on how best to support families or crack down on crime. Yet there are clear principles that we can all draw from Scripture. This provides some much needed common ground for all Christians: the uniqueness of every human being, the central role of families and parenting, a focus on the poor and disadvantaged, the need for integrity in public life, to name just some. So we are just beginning to develop our cross-party relationships of trust and friendship to provoke debate on important issues and so make a difference. We also want to say to the Church: wake up – bring to an end the ridiculous divisions and petty rivalries and get together, in every town and village and community. Come together, find one another in a new way, build relationships across boundaries and through insecurities and begin a new dialogue with those around you. If we can come together over deep party-political divides, why can't all of us, however we view and do church? There is a world waiting to hear from those of us who hold the keys to the meaning of life, but in our division and apathy we have not recently earned the right to be heard.

Apart from any desire to act collectively, we are all primarily involved in trying to make the policies pursued by our own parties to be based more on biblical values. The Conservative Christian Fellowship has grown in numbers, strength and influence over the years until it now genuinely influences party policy in a more Christ-like direction. We have developed a policy wing called the 'Renewing One Nation' unit to pursue practical policy ideas to help us to find new ways of pushing back the frontiers of poverty. The Fellowship has also been successful in encouraging and supporting more and more Christians to become actively engaged in the party.

In conjunction with friends in the Labour and Liberal Democrat parties. We have also launched an initiative called 'Christians in Politics', a venture designed to encourage believers from all backgrounds and walks of life, whatever their denomination, to become engaged in the political process and to try and make a positive difference. The message is simple: don't just sit on the sidelines, moaning at the state of British politics. Get engaged by joining a party – in accordance with your outlook on life – and work for change. Politicians make big decisions affecting all of our lives. No political party is perfect, and our gospel is so much greater than any human ideology, but we should not underestimate the good we can do by entering this important battleground.

It used to be thought that if Christians got involved at all it was only to bang on about homosexuality, abortion and marriage. Times are changing. Although those issues may remain important, there is a growing revelation that God is concerned for so much more. Let me list just a fraction: the absence of security for so many children as a result of the breakdown of parental relationships, the terrifying spread of drugs and a gun culture, the dangers to children from the easy access that the internet has provided for perverted minds, the ethical boundaries for genetic engineering and euthanasia, and finding new ways to create global stability and prosperity. The debate is changing, the pillar of cloud and fire is moving on. It is time for Christians to get out of the obsolete trenches dug for a completely different era and take up new weapons of warfare and engagement fit for the 21st century. A new day is dawning in Britain. There is a vacuum in the public square, and vacuums do not remain unfilled for long. The Church must decide whether it is prepared to lay aside old paradigms and prejudices and learn a new way to serve.

Keep us, Lord, so awake in the duties of our calling that we may sleep in thy peace and wake in thy glory.

John Donne

If you give a man a fish, he will eat once.
If you teach a man to fish, he will eat for the rest of his life.
If you are thinking a year ahead, sow seed.
If you are thinking ten years ahead, plant a tree.
If you are thinking one hundred years ahead,
    educate the people.
By sowing seed, you will harvest once.
By planting a tree, you will harvest tenfold.
By educating the people you will harvest one hundredfold.

Kuantzu

People become house builders through building houses, harp players through playing the harp. We grow to be just by doing things which are just.

Aristotle

Father, source of all power, we confess that we do not always use the powers you have given us as you intend. Sometimes we are afraid of the power we wield, and so do not use it at all; at other times we are careless in our use of it and harm others; at yet other times we deliberately misuse it to achieve our own selfish ends. We confess our misuse of our God-given powers, and ask your grace to use them properly in future.

We think of the power of the nations of the world. In international affairs it so often seems that events are out of our control, and rule us. Father, help us to see how national power can be wielded for the fulfilment of your will.

We think of the power of governments. They now touch our personal lives at so many points. Father, may politicians and civil servants use their powers responsibly and respect the rights of individuals.

Give us the courage to challenge them when they are wrong, and willingness to share in the processes of government ourselves. May the power of governments everywhere be used for the good of all.

Father, yours is the ultimate power. We see evidence of it everywhere in the world, but most of all in Jesus Christ. In him we see the power of your love: weakness and death did not destroy him and you raised him from death. May that same power of love be in us.

Caryl Micklem

O Lord, I remember before thee tonight all
   the workers of the world:
Workers with hand or brain:
Workers in cities or in the fields . . .
Employers and employees:
Those who command and those who obey:
Those whose work is dangerous:
Those whose work is monotonous or mean:
Those who can find no work to do:
Those whose work is the service of the poor
Or the healing of the sick
Or the proclamation of the gospel of Christ
At home or in foreign places.

John Baillie

Goodness is love in action, love with its hand to the
plough, love with the burden on its back, love following
his footsteps who went about continually doing good.

J. Hamilton

*Give us, O Lord, true humility, a meek and quiet spirit, a
loving, friendly, holy and useful manner of life. Help us to
bear the burdens of our neighbours and to be prepared for
every good work.*

Jeremy Taylor

Primacy of love for God and human beings is the characteristic of every real Christian witness. This is the acid test of sincerity. It is the beginning and ending of all Christian heritage in politics. By this yardstick we measure every policy and programme, for only when love decides our attitude is our programme even likely to be right . . . This is the true greatness for Christians that by the practice of Jesus' ethic of love we make ourselves the servants of all.

George Thomas

Don't waste life in doubts and fears; spend yourself on the work before you, well assured that the right performance of this hour's duties will be the best preparation for the hours or ages that follow it.

Ralph Waldo Emerson

I am tired in the Lord's work, but not tired of it.

George Whitefield

You asked for my hands
that you might use them for your purpose.
I gave them for a moment then withdrew them
for the work was hard.

You asked for my mouth
to speak out against injustice.
I gave you a whisper that I might not be accused.

You asked for my eyes
to see the pain of poverty.
I closed them for I did not want to see.

You asked for my life
that you might work through me.
I gave a small part that I might not get too involved.

Lord, forgive my calculated efforts to serve you,
only when it is convenient for me to do so,
only in those places where it is safe to do so,
and only with those who make it easy to do so.

Father, forgive me,
renew me,
send me out
as a usable instrument
that I might take seriously
the meaning of your cross.

                                        Joe Seremane

A Day in the Life

Ken Russell

Rank Wharfedale, Yorkshire

January 1962
The end of my first week. It seems I'm expected to be an expert on some very specialised areas of engineering that are quite new to me. I also have a new language to learn – Yorkshire. On the shop-floor particularly I need an interpreter! The Works Manager, who knows of my Christian faith, chummily called me something that was unintelligible to me. Today I was misguided enough to use the same in return, at which he dissolved, helpless. It appears that vulgarity scarcely describes it. Ah well. Perhaps Wesley would have included it in 'sins of ignorance and surprise'.

February 1962
I think I'm learning. At first I was severe on my new staff who were not pulling their weight. Reflecting on a discussion in the Church Fellowship, which suggested that Jesus seemed to get the best out of some unlikely characters, I've been looking into their motivation. One has serious domestic problems; the other a hefty chip on his shoulder. I'm not much of a counsellor, but giving

one extra time off, and listening to the other, seems to have helped.

March 1962
I've taken to staying late to deal with technical correspondence. It gives me peace and quiet, and, anyway, I'm still living in a hotel until I can find a house for the family. Nellie*, the cook, brings me coffee and sandwiches before she leaves. She is a Salvation Army girl and a bundle of fun and joy, a great advertisement for Christianity. Her cooking is equally robust!

February 1965
I'm becoming increasingly conscious of the value of keeping time for daily prayer. It seems particularly effective if it's early in the morning, although I sometimes fit it in with my drive to work, or when shovelling snow to get to the car! It does seem to make for clearer thinking and greater calmness. Including my staff and colleagues in prayers helps me to see them differently.

November 1967
I leave on Monday, at short notice again, for a tour of several countries for technical discussions and meetings with partners and suppliers. Looks as though I'll only just be back for Christmas. I'm conscious of not spending enough time with the boys because of the hours I am working. Fortunately Barbara understands about the demands of a responsible job. I must at least see them playing football on Saturday, and perhaps the Lord will forgive me if I take them swimming on Sunday.

June 1968
Personnel brought me a student for a month's experience in the lab. First impressions were not encouraging. He had a leather jacket, a Mohican haircut – multicoloured to boot – and rings in unexpected places. Worse, he is known as 'Spike'. We had a long conversation. He is quiet, well-spoken, well-adjusted, dedicated to electronics engineering and clearly set for a distinguished career. May be prudent to keep him out of sight during the Chairman's visit next week. Sorry, Spike!

September 1970
Bill Young, of the main Board, joined us for lunch today. He told us that during the previous week Lord Rank had dropped in to the boardroom, and talked for an hour about the Holy Spirit. Apparently he held them spellbound. Bill at least seems to have been affected. He is thinking seriously of retiring early to undertake some voluntary work. Well done, J. Arthur – and the Holy Spirit!

October 1974
It's a relief to be back in Tokyo after the lecture tour. Today was free, and I was taken to see the Buddhist Temples at Nikko. Magnificent. The Yomeimon Gate is also called 'Higurashi-mon', which apparently translates as 'You can look at it for a whole day without exhausting its wonders'! One word can say so much, like 'love' or 'the cross'. The rich adornments of Buddhism and the simplicity of Shinto are reflected in our own churches; some people want to offer their finest craftsmanship to God, while others want no distraction in worship.

May 1975
Personnel have a problem with one of my engineers, which now becomes my problem. Richard Chang has only a student's entry visa. They failed to check. Now it has expired. Do I wish to keep him? Yes, I do; he is leading an important development project. I asked him to see me and explain himself. After some flannelling, it seems that he expected us to offer a back-hander to an 'official' and the right papers would magically appear. He has a lot to learn, some of it painful. Meanwhile he has had a stinging lecture from me. I'm fortunate that occasions for really harsh words are rare.

July 1975
Another serious problem in Final Assembly. Fred Maynard, their Shop Steward, has been causing trouble. Output has suffered when we can ill afford it. No doubt the timing was chosen deliberately. The Shop Foreman would like to sack him, but that is not realistic. My test-rig builder is retiring next month, and I believe Maynard has the skills necessary. I offered to take him, which will mean his relinquishing his Union post. Personnel will say that they will tell him he was hand-picked for the job. They have no conscience.

April 1977
The Christian Fellowship in the factory has given me a standing invitation to join them in their lunch-hour meetings. It is only rarely that I can, as the factory has a different lunch hour. Today the speaker was a passionate Pentecostalist but the content did not seem to relate much to the real world. I don't think the members of the Fellowship meet resentment on the shop floor. It may sometimes be ill-advised to indulge in evangelism in

the factory, but I wonder if one of them might just be a rock for someone to turn to if disaster strikes.

May 1977
I'm not the flavour of the month in Production. The lines will be cleared for the M-type System in eight weeks, but I can't release drawings to Production Engineering yet. The development models meet the specification, but I don't consider them good enough. Customers would, I think, be short-changed. It isn't anyone's fault, and we are nearly there. Some materials which don't uniformly obey the laws of physics require a lengthy iterative approach. Lord, keep us all calm.

November 1980
We lose Padmini today; her baby is due shortly. She has been a good engineer. She achieved second place in the National 'Woman Engineer of the Year' awards for her work on one of our projects. When I first appointed her I was pleased that there was no prejudice regarding her sex or her Sri Lankan nationality. Am I too proud of my team?

March 1981
Another batch of redundancies announced. Some are old friends. One came to me as lab assistant. He was so good that I got him onto an ONC day-release course and as a result he went on to university with a bursary I was able to arrange. He graduated two years ago and took a responsible job in Production. Today he received his redundancy notice. Praying for him is not enough. I have some telephoning to do.

151

June 1982

With the sale of our company by Rank, I do not feel that I want to join the new owners, partly because I should like to do some specific Christian service before I retire. I shall miss the technical exchanges of life in the lab. I am fortunate to have worked in such an exciting field. The progress made in electronics has been breathtaking. I believe that I've learnt something new on just about every working day for more than 30 years. I feel slightly guilty that work has been such fun!

St. Winifred's, Christian Endeavour Guest House

July 1984

Took the excursion to Criccieth. Lovely day, so went in for a swim. As I was crossing the prom I overtook Mrs. Lambert, supported by two friends. It was clearly a struggle for the three of them. I jokingly said to Mrs. Lambert, 'Coming in for a dip?' Later her friends told me that she had won international gold medals for swimming. It was humbling, and it reminded me that many frail and elderly guests could tell of similar achievements. Appearance is no basis for judgement.

October 1988

Anne Walker died during the night. Called in the doctor and Coroner's Officer about 2 this morning. The Walkers had been coming for many years – a very private couple. I let George use the office for making phone calls and sat with him off and on for most of the day. It was my first experience of offering support so soon after a bereavement. He talked, and I learned of a remarkable life of service to his town, where he had been made

Mayor last year. Mostly he talked of Anne. They had met first in Sunday school and had been married for 55 years. She had been his inspiration.

May 1989
I should not have favourite guests, but I was delighted to have John and Margaret Fisher with us again this week. John was pastor of a large Baptist Church; now retired and looking after a house-church in a small village. He had been offered a prestigious post in an American theological seminary but turned it down because he felt his house-church would miss him.

July 1990
Some evening prayers and devotional meetings are led by the guests. Often they are an inspiration. This evening was like that. It occurred to me a few weeks ago that I never hear the element of confession in a guest's prayers. Since then I have been particularly observant. Confession is rare. I wonder if it is overlooked in their enthusiasm for praise and thanksgiving, or whether they don't sin on holiday! Perhaps some consider penitence unnecessary after conversion. It's made me more aware of the need for confession in my prayers.

April 1991
One of the guests asked me today, 'What denomination are you?' I actually had to think before I replied. In all my time here no one else has asked me, and I can't remember asking it of any of the guests. It seems irrelevant. Our Easter morning Communion service in the house must embrace a very wide spectrum of Christian conviction and affiliation, but all share without

reserve. Mealtimes often seem to take on a eucharistic quality.

* * * * * *

September 2003
Looking back on it all, I wish I had done many things better, made fewer mistakes, been a more effective witness for Jesus Christ. For his part, though he never solved any of my technical problems, he was there whenever I needed him, which was many times each day. As an engineer, I needed teaching by him that people are more important than technology. I am grateful that he chose to do it through a loving family at home and in the Church, and through those many admirable colleagues I shall always recall with affection.

*   Names have been changed for confidentiality.

154

I was particularly anxious during my period of office to cultivate my relationships with the engineering bodies and faculties. As often as not it is the engineer who puts the results of science to practical use. Moreover, whilst the scientist may be the intellectual of the numerate world, the engineer is the artist. All design, like all policy, is a compromise between divergent requirements – safety and cost, mobility and strength, speed and reliability, and so forth. It requires a touch of artistic genius to get the balance right. This is the function of the design engineer, whether he is producing a bridge, a motor car, a radar station, a military aircraft, or a safety razor.

Lord Hailsham

Make a careful use of your fragments of time. It is wonderful how much can be got through by these means. A great deal of study, or writing, or other work, can be done by a resolute will in odd quarters of hours, and very often we can get no more. Nothing is more commonly said than that if you want something done, you will have a much better chance of getting it done by a busy person than by an idle one, and this simply because the former has learnt the secret of economising his or her time.

Walsham How

Lord, I get so busy.
Sometimes because I want to help.
Sometimes because I can't say no.
Sometimes because I'm flattered to be asked.
And it all adds up to strain, to tiredness,
to not having two minutes to call my own.
And then comes the bad temper, the resentment.
And before long I'm hating the people who asked me.
Hating the people who want my help.
And then I feel guilty, and I hate them more.

Lord, I feel like a mouse in a treadmill.
Rushing around, faster and faster.
Getting nowhere.
And the first thing that goes out of the window
is you.
No time, Lord, sorry!
Then my family.
They should know I'm busy and not ask for my time!
And my friends.
Can't they see all the things I have to do?

Lord. It's at times like this that I need you most.
Yet you seem so far away.
Why, Lord? Where have you gone?
Then I hear it, the quiet voice . . .
. . . be still and know that I am God.
You *are* near. You have been all the time.
And I understand
that I can't hear you if I don't listen.
That I will feel alone if I don't give time to you.
Lord, I just thought so much depended on me.
I know the whole world wouldn't end if I took a break,
but it made me feel important.
I need to remember that it's your world, your work.
I'm glad to have a part in it, but it's yours, not mine.
And when I've done what I can,
I can safely leave the rest to you.

Lord, still my heart.
Help me cut down the adrenalin.
Give me your peace.

Eddie Askew
A Silence and a Shouting

O God, I am Mustafah the tailor and I work at the shop of Muhammad Ali. The whole day long I sit and pull the needle and the thread through the cloth. O God, you are the needle and I am the thread. I am attached to you and I follow you. When the thread tries to slip away from the needle it becomes tangled and must be cut so that it can be put back in the right place. O God, help me to follow you wherever you may lead me. For I am really only Mustafah the tailor, and I work at the shop of Muhammad Ali on the great square.

A Muslim's first prayer as a Christian

The day is there and the sunshine,
With steamers in the harbour,
But is there work?
Others have friends,
Others have money.
They can drain their whisky bottle,
And I stand nearby unemployed.
Dear God, can't you give me work in the harbour?
To have money for wife and children.
To put my little bit in your basket next Sunday.
Please give me work, good Lord Jesus.
We praise you.

Prayer of a Ghanaian harbour man out of work

In a culture oriented toward leisure, we tend to undervalue work or to value it solely as a means of making money. Feelings about ordinary, unexciting tasks can increase, especially when such tasks seem to steal time we would rather use for leisure activities. Many people feel trapped by unrewarding responsibilities and by jobs not valued by others. [St.] Benedict invites us to consider work well done and with attention as a gift of gratitude to God. He tells us to let go of resentment, to see our tasks as opportunities, to express with thanksgiving and as a means of service to those around us.

Elizabeth J. Canham

Our hands are not machines
in the factories of profit,
our bodies are not just robots
for production of wealth.

Our lives are given dignity
by God
not by possessions,
our dreams achieve their
quality in freedom
not control.

Our job is joy
our labour creation
our business peace,
our task to be.
Be with us, Lord, in rest and work.
Our hope is to live life
and to live it to the full.

Linda Jones, CAFOD

My Christian Journey

Una Chandler

Through many dangers, toils and snares
I have already come.

John Newton

I was brought up in a poor Christian family in the West
Indies. We had a strong faith in God and all we hoped
for was to worship him and for him to guide us.
Sometimes we scarcely had a meal on our table, and we
had to rely on God for strength as we went about our
daily lives. I can look back now and thank God and my
family; for my experience has helped me and taught me
how to live my life by faith, hope and trust in the Lord.

When we arrived in England, my husband and I began
worship at a black-led Pentecostal church. However,
after the death of my husband in 1982, I felt that my
whole world had fallen apart. While worshipping, I felt
isolated and alone with the hurt of bereavement and I
found myself praying and crying out to God in despair
and anger as I questioned my feelings about him.

One night while I was asleep, God visited me in a dream,
where I saw myself standing outside the doors of the

then West Reading Methodist Church. I obeyed the call of God as I journeyed into unfamiliar surroundings, with people I didn't know. It is with hindsight that I can look back and see that through worshipping at this new church, God was able to call me to be a lay preacher. My Christian journey has since continued to be one of excitement, fun, laughter, and sometimes sadness and tears.

Each year I am always keen to watch the London Marathon, and as the athletes prepare and train to run the race, that's how I see myself on this journey, taking part in a learning process, step by step each day learning more about God.

When Jesus told his disciples to go into all the world and preach his gospel to all nations (Matthew 28:18-20), he also sent them out filled with the Holy Spirit to seek souls for his kingdom, which began a journey without an end. Significantly, this is how I feel about my role as a workplace Chaplain at Reading Borough Council.

At work colleagues sometimes share with me what life is like for them, their everyday stresses and problems with family life, asking, like so many of us, how they can cope with it all. How do we cope when everything around us seems at times impossible? When I began the role as Chaplain I prayed and asked for God's guidance, that he would grant me the words of wisdom, knowledge and understanding to be able to share my Christian faith with people. I have learnt in my experience that it's not so much bringing men or women to my place of worship, but it's telling them that God loves them just as they are, and that he died for me and also for them.

I am also conscious of the condition of our world – a world full of hurt, pain and sorrow. As I listen to those around me, I can hear their despair and anger. As Christians we have a responsibility to reach out a hand of compassion to all humankind and to help others to understand that God's love is special, and that it's everlasting.

As a single parent, a mother and grandmother of two, a Chaplain to my local council, volunteer in a local charity shop, and also as a lay preacher, the journey can become tiresome and lonely. Nevertheless, I cannot stop for a rest; I must go as the Spirit of God leads me. I meet up with ordinary people, people who are always ready to share their concerns. I listen, speak and I try to show forth the love of God to Christians and non-Christians, as they seek a better way of life.

For this journey and for the everyday problems of life, I must have patience, endurance, courage and confidence. With God in my mind I have a vision for a better world where his presence, love and joy bring a message of peace.

I do not know when or where my Christian journey will end, but I am sure that 'my help comes from the Lord, who made heaven and earth' (Psalm 121:2). Thanks be to God who has given me the victory through him.

The Lord is my Pace Setter – I shall not rush –
He makes me stop for quiet intervals.
He provides me with images of stillness which
   restore my serenity.
He leads me in ways of efficiency through calmness
   of mind
And his guidance is Peace.

Even though I have a great many things to
   accomplish each day,
I will not fret.
For his presence is here.
His kindness now, his all-importance, will keep me
   in balance.
He prepares refreshment and renewal in the midst of
   my activity.
By anointing my mind with his oils of tranquillity,
My cup of joyous energy overflows.
Truly harmony and effectiveness shall be the fruits of
   my hours,
For I shall work in the pace of my Lord
And dwell in his house for ever.

Anonymous

Many people find attuning to grace easy in the morning, their sense of God enlivened by the beauty of nature or the gift of life itself, but more difficult as they enter the busyness of the work-day. But some have found ways to bless moments at work. 'I've made an act of inward blessing out of greeting my co-workers as I come in for the day,' explained one office worker. 'Just the acts of smiling, greeting people warmly, asking about a continuing family matter give me a chance to pray God's blessing on them in my heart. That blessing also means she's better connected to them as part of the team through the day. One personnel manager said, 'My job is really like that of a symphony conductor; I've got to help people to work together harmoniously. So I offer the intention to do that as I come in at the beginning of the day and hold the image in my mind of conducting an orchestra. Then when I feel I'm losing track during the day, I come back to that prayer-image.'

Robert Corin Morris

The men and women who have best interpreted God to their fellows in the past have, as a rule, been extraordinary people, who have become extraordinary through their nearness to God.

E. Burroughs

The chairman of the Education Committee moved that the resolutions on his minutes should be approved and confirmed. The newly appointed alderman rose and complained about the cutting down of maintenance allowances to scholarship and free place holders . . .

The Mental Hospital business appropriately followed that of the Education Committee. Again Alderman Astell was dissatisfied. Again Lovell Brown felt the chill of disillusionment creeping across his heart.

Without emotion, without haste, without even, as far as Lovell could discern, any noticeable interest, the South Riding County Council ploughed through its agenda. The General mumbled; the clerk shuffled papers, the chairmen of committees answered desultory questions.

Lovell had come expectant of drama, indignation, combat, amusement, shock. He found boredom and monotony.

Disillusion chastened him.

Winifred Holtby

Nurture great thoughts, for you will never go higher than your thoughts.

Benjamin Disraeli

Creator of rainbows,
Come through the closed doors
of our emotions, mind and imagination;
come alongside us as we walk,
come to us at work and worship,
come to our meetings and councils,
come and call us by name,
call us to pilgrimage.

Wounded healer,
out of our disunity
may we be re-membered,
out of pain of our division
may we see your glory.
Call us from present
pre-occupation
to future community.

Spirit of Unity,
challenge our preconceptions,
enable us to grow in love and understanding,
accompany us on our journey together,
that we may go out with confidence
into your world as a new creation –
one body in you,
that the world may believe.

Kate McIlhagga

All service ranks the same with God. It is not what your daily work is, but the spirit in which you are doing it. God asks from us all that we should discover all the resources of our personality, mobilise them into activity and dedicate them to his service. If a road sweeper does this, he is serving God, and pleasing God as much as the archbishop who does this, and more than the archbishop who does not.

. . . So fear not, lowly toiler in the job you don't much like. God has not forgotten you. You may be selling clothes to difficult customers, looking after someone else's children . . . you may be doing what some ignorant people call menial work. You may long for recognition and find it not. You may nurse sick, irritable people, or pack butter into boxes, or teach grubby schoolboys. You are to try to see your job as service to the community and service to God. Do *your* job as well as it can be done by you. It is only required in stewards that they be found *faithful*.

Leslie Weatherhead

The energy of Love discharges itself along the lines which form a triangle whose points are God, self and neighbour.

C. F. Dodd

You in your small corner . . .

Dyfed Matthews

Making for the refectory, down the long corridor, I side-stepped a number of students. We all had one thing on our minds . . . food! Most students in Further Ed., together with lecturers, skip a decent breakfast, preferring an extra few minutes in bed; so by lunch-time everyone is ravenous! These were the days before fast food was invented yet we could make a fair-sized lunch disappear in less than ten minutes.

On this occasion I had something else on my mind. I was trying to get the few Christian students prepared to meet in the lunch break to come together to hear Rita Nightingale.[1] In 1977 Rita was arrested at Bangkok Airport and found to have over three kilos of heroin in her baggage. Despite her innocence she was detained and eventually sentenced to 20 years in prison. After three years she was released following a royal pardon from the king of Thailand. While in prison she became a Christian. Her story was nothing short of a miracle. Perhaps these teenagers would listen to her and realise for the first time, maybe, that God is real and can be personally known in Jesus. About 30 students turned up and a few stayed behind to ask questions of our guest. The meeting had been a success!

As a lecturer, helping students to organise themselves and run a Christian Union in a Further Education College has its own frustrations and rewards but, looking back, this was not just a matter of personal witness in the workplace; it was a God-given opportunity to help students to take the first steps towards knowing and serving God. Over the 20 years of support for a Christian presence in the college many lives were influenced for good and leaders of some present-day churches grown.

College life for those with faith is by no means easy. Young people arrive in College trying to establish for themselves an independent lifestyle. It is a time of new challenges to thought and behaviour patterns. Decisions about money, relationships, career and responsibilities all have to be made. The parental strings are loosened and this in itself puts pressure on teenagers to try out everything new. The trial and error process is a more profound learning experience for some than the actual course for which they have enrolled!

It is precisely because of these life issues coming together for the majority of students that Christians in a college have such great responsibility. They are right at the cutting edge of Christian living. It is sink or swim for them! This is particularly evident when they decide to join the Christian Union. The young Christian, just finding their feet in making God-honouring choices, is now faced with a fiery furnace and a lions' den! The greatest pressure is from friends. Will identifying with the Christian Union result in loss of friendship and derision? It is a real dilemma for some.

The Christian students who choose to identify with the Christian Union are some of the bravest Christians around. What they lose in worldly status is more than made up for in Christian fellowship and support which continues often long beyond college days.

Staff support for young Christians in college can be something like life on a lonely planet. Many times meetings have been arranged to find that only one or two students turn up! If a speaker from outside the college is visiting this can be an enormous embarrassment. Sometimes students arrive late, misbehave or just want a break from their routine and have little interest in the point of the meeting! One sometimes wonders why the Lord has placed one in such a situation. Could it be a test of one's own faith?

In most years the Christian Union is like a weak and tender plant and can easily be blown about! I recall one occasion when the college had an influx of Malaysian students. Would there be a Christian/Muslim conflict? Would it be right to invite followers of Islam to the meetings? And what if they came? The Malaysian students solved the problem for the Christians! If Christians could meet for their prayers, why could the Malaysians not be given a room in which to pray? Appeals were made to the principal and out rolled the prayer mats! There was some friendly dialogue, however. These same Malaysian students readily received a Christmas gift of a colourful booklet produced by the Scripture Gift Mission, in Arabic!

In 1992 the Christian Union became more established in the college. Rather than depending upon the efforts of Christian staff to support it, the vision to have a College Outreach Worker, someone to stand alongside the CU, became a reality. Local churches and individuals supported the Worker financially and in prayer. The Universities and Colleges Christian Fellowship helped to co-ordinate the work and soon a pattern of leadership was established which provided continuity for students.

Now, well over a decade of Christian witness has taken place in the college. The lives of CU leaders have been influenced for good; some going on to be leaders of CUs in universities; others taking up training in Bible Colleges for Christian service round the world; some simply pursuing their own careers in any number of fields. The workplace opportunities for Christian witness in a college can be limited but in this case remarkable results have occurred through staying firmly with the vision until it became reality.

Being a lecturer is clearly a calling but it is no different from any other sphere of work. I believe that every Christian who works is strategically placed by God. There are great challenges to one's faith and witness but also great blessings for those who are faithful and prepared to follow the Lord's leading. As William Carey put it: 'Attempt good things for God; expect great things from God.'

Jesus, our Lord, said to his disciples, 'You are the light of the world . . . let your light shine.' While it is true that we can organise events for God in the workplace where there is opportunity, if we simply live as Christians our

171

witness will overflow from our life. Witness is not only something we do but it is something we are. However, this does not mean we can shirk or fail to recognise our God-given opportunities.

It has been said that if we are serious about workplace witness the Holy Spirit will give us the opportunity to share the reason for the hope that is within us. How true that proved to be in this 'small corner'!

1   The story of Rita Nightingale is recounted in *Freed for Life*, Hodder & Stoughton.

Can we not say to the young apprentice who has just learnt the use of a high precision lathe, and is thrilled at his new ability to use so apparently heavy and bulky a machine to prepare a piece of metal to a given shape with an accuracy of one ten-thousandth of an inch, that God is equally thrilled, and that his sheer joy in the situation is not wholly different from that of the angels who behold God's glory and rejoice?

C. A. Coulson

I took the list [of chemicals] and looked at it, not understanding a word of what was written, and made my way to the department where all the chemicals were stored, hoping that someone might rescue me and weigh up all the various chemicals and reagents. I could find no one to assist me so I decided to go back and face the music . . . When I told my new boss that I knew nothing about chemistry, he was quite cross and rather taken aback. 'How did you get in here, who sent you here?' I explained how I had been interviewed and he stormed off to find the professor who had interviewed me in London, leaving me with a book to read which was far out of my depth.

E. Jack Mitchell

The more competitive a society becomes, the more prevalent are the aspirations to succeed. The higher the possible summit of achievement is perceived, the more frequent will be the relegation to the foothills. It is not surprising that depression and suicide risk are high amongst university students. Conditions of high unemployment will spawn the incidence of depressive illness. The world of work has for long provided a sense of self-worth and esteem which, once removed, leaves the redundant, and those who have never worked, aimless, depressed, and without confidence, even if rewarded financially for the loss of role.

Anthony Hulbert

Grant, O Lord, to all teachers and students, to know that which is worth knowing, to love that which is worth loving, to praise that which pleaseth thee most, to esteem that which is most precious unto thee, and to dislike whatsoever is evil in thine eyes.

Thomas à Kempis

Success is to be measured not so much by the position that one has reached in life, as by the obstacles [a person] has overcome while trying to succeed.

Booker T. Washington

When I heard the learn'd astronomer,
When the proofs, the figures, were ranged
	in columns before me,
When I was shown the charts and diagrams, to add,
	divide and measure them,
When I sitting heard the astronomer where he lectured
	with much applause in the lecture room,
How soon unaccountable I became tired and sick,
Till rising and gliding out I wandered off by myself,
In the mystical moist night-air, and from time to time,
Look'd up in perfect silence at the stars.

Walt Whitman

All the youngsters served an apprenticeship in the net
store in Newlyn, learning how to make up the gear, slice
steel wire, and put a trawl together. Then we were let
loose on the high seas . . . During my first twelve months
at sea full time, things improved. But painfully slowly. I
felt squeamish every trip, and the tightening in my
stomach every time I knew it was time to go below to
chop ice took a long time to disappear . . . The deck was
no happier place. Cowhides were used on the bottom of
the nets to stop them being chafed to death on the
seabed. When the nets came in it was my task to climb
right inside to check for holes. The stench from these
cowhides as they dried was unbelievable.

Roger Nowell

[So] often we make plans without laying them before God. Or, if we do bring them before the Lord we prescribe the solution to him without waiting upon him to direct us. We just want God to rubber-stamp our hasty decisions. The result of all this is feverish activity on our part. We go to bed late, we get up early. We burn the candle at both ends and we put a huge strain upon ourselves (depression, headaches, heart attacks); we put pressure on our marriages (affairs, arguments, divorce); and we neglect our children (wrong relationships, drug and alcohol abuse, insecurity). We defend our behaviour by protesting that all this hard work was for the sake of the family: 'I was earning the money for you . . .' But the outcome has told another story. There is a poignant motto in the Book of Proverbs: 'Better is a dinner of vegetables where love is than a fattened ox with hatred in it' (Proverbs 15:17).

James Jones

May every task be done with joy
And every word that we employ
Show the Lord in Heaven above
That all we do, we do for love.

Gormola Kernewek

What stillness and silence do is to help us reflect at a deeper level, to get in touch with our inner selves, which are really our true selves. We can only do this in solitude because the rest of our lives are conducted at a completely different, if you like surface, level. There our lives are governed by feelings, the daily complexities of living are dealt with by instant decisions or emotional responses, and we find ourselves so often blown like leaves along a path by the winds of the world's bustle. As we career along, can we really be having a true say in what we're doing or where we're going? When the answer is no, perhaps it's because people have lost touch with their true selves and I feel sure that this is the cause of many a breakdown, depression or mid-life crisis.

Delia Smith

We can never know God's power unless we attempt the impossible. As long as we are doing things that are within our capabilities, things for which we are qualified and skilled, we can too easily trust our own gifts (forgetting that those come from God also). Only when we try to do things beyond us will we end our attempts at power, dependently turn to the Lord, and rely solely on him.

Marva J. Dawn

177

Politicans are God's Ministers

Donald Gray

Just before the dissolution of the 1990 Parliament I claimed the privilege of preaching to MPs at a Valedictory Service for retiring members. Not least I was sensitive to a comment made by Speaker Boothroyd that there are few opportunities these days for members to hear the Chaplain preach.

That is true. Each sitting day the Chaplain prays in the chamber before the start of business but, in days gone by, sermons were preached regularly before Parliament. The House marked various days (if they were in session) with a sermon in St. Margaret's ('the Parish Church of the House of Commons'): 5th November, 30th January (martyrdom of Charles I), 29th May (Restoration of Charles II), together with the anniversary of the Sovereign's Accession and other General Fast and Thanksgiving Days.

At the beginning of my address I admitted to a certain nervousness, because I knew that in 1772 it was proposed in the House that the sermon (thankfully only the sermon) should be publicly burnt by the Common Hangman as containing 'arbitrary, tory, high flown doctrine'. But at least I was able to assure members that there would not be a repeat of the events of 17th November 1640. On that occasion reinforcements were brought in: there were two preachers.

> Tuesday was a fast day which was kept piously and devoutly; Doctor Burgess and Master Marshall preached before the House of Commons at least 7 hours betwixt them.

I was briefer! In my sermon my aim was to encourage retiring members to leave Westminster with a sense of satisfaction: not over-weaning self-satisfaction, but a sense of duty fulfilled. I realised that none of them would take with them a full tally of successes; there are always many failures and disappointments, sins both of commission and omission. The *Prayer Book* has it right: we repent of 'things we ought to have done and things we ought not to have done'.

The Palace of Westminster has its own weekly journal, amusingly called *The House Magazine*. Shortly before I preached, there had been a series in it by retiring MPs entitled 'Thoughts before Going' which had revealed a whole variety of attitudes towards the approach of the end of a parliamentary career. I told that congregation of MPs I now wanted to offer them one particular thought before they went.

It was no more, perhaps, than they expected, that I should speak my mind on this occasion, but there were, nevertheless, many quizzical looks when I told them, without equivocation, that for the past 10, 20, 30 or more years they had all been 'ministers of God'. Now, how do you work that out, you may also ask?

Well, I start from the proposition that this world is God's world, and that not only did he create it, he recreated it through the incarnation of our Lord Jesus Christ. 'Incarnation' is not just a fancy theological word, it is a very political word. It is one which I wish spin doctors would more often pinch from us than phrases like 'broad church', which is usually employed with no sense of its historical background. 'Incarnation' in this sense means becoming human – in the flesh – in *this* world. Incidentally, the writers of creeds (in Greek) were PC before their day – they said that 'Jesus became *human'* – not just 'man'!

What I want to say is this: the message (not just a once-a-year message for Christmas) is that God thought this world *so* important that he chose to come to it himself – and in human form. Not as a sham or pretence; not pretending to be human, and really being an angel or a spook (or anything like that) but taking on our human flesh. Now, from that point on, human life has never been the same; this world has never been the same. Because of this fact our fellow human beings should never again be abused, patronised, ignored or dealt with cruelly, indifferently, casually, scornfully. Because now they share with us the dignity of Christ. To abuse them is to abuse Christ. Equally this wonderful world of ours, and its amazing resources, should never be squandered, wasted, distorted, unequally shared, because this is God's cradle, God's throne.

My task as Chaplain to the Speaker was always firmly non-party, but *not* non-political. I believed I had an important task to affirm the high, important and significant role of the politician. Because what does the House of Commons (or any other democratic parliament) exist for, except to order the affairs of God's world and his children within it?

Now, I realise that some Members of Parliament might reasonably protest: 'I don't share your Christian premise.' Fair enough, I wouldn't want to deprive them of their right to their own opinion, but that does not alter the situation. The task is performed, even by those who choose not to recognise it.

However, let me make one thing clear: the fact that politicians are God's ministers does not in any way lessen the weighty responsibilities of the office. It sets the matter in its context, but it does not for one moment reduce the need for God's grace in performing their duties. Politicians are God's ministers, not his puppets. He doesn't pull the strings, and they perform. In his infinite love God does not deprive any of us of our free will. His love is so great that he waits for us freely to choose to serve his purposes.

Yet God never deserts his servants. He expects much of them, but as St. Paul said, 'God keeps faith and will not let you be tested beyond your powers.' In the light of that I was able to say to those MPs who were leaving that they should go knowing that they had been performing a God-given task and that they should be aware that their role and task had been acknowledged and affirmed. It is equally the message to all those who continue to serve as members.

Over my years in the House, members would regularly come up to me with a worried question: 'Chaplain, why do you pray at the end of Prayers each day that God might "prevent" us?' Old hands knew that the words really mean *prae-venire*, that is, 'Go before'. However, one of my last actions, with the encouragement of Speaker Boothroyd, was to change that collect so that it became 'Go before us, O Lord'.

That collect continues to be prayed for all members (either in their presence or in their absence) every day when Parliament sits, as it has since 1661; that God might 'go before us':

> Go before us, O Lord, in all our doings
> with thy most gracious favour
> and further us with thy continual help,
> that in all our works, begun, continued
> and ended in thee,
> we may glorify thy Holy Name,
> and finally by thy mercy
> obtain everlasting life,
> through Jesus Christ our Lord. Amen.

Back in 1997 I told those retiring members: 'You have served, I trust, as faithful stewards and ministers of his will – and God has gone before you in this and all your doings. His help will be with you so that all your works (now and in the future) may begin, continue and eventually end with his almighty blessing.'

Equally I continue to pray that that same blessing rests on our Parliament today. I encourage you to add your prayers to mine.

I have not been unsuccessful in politics, but if I had to do it again, I would invest my life in people rather than in programmes.

George Lansbury

O God, when the heart is warmest,
And the head is clearest,
Give me to act:
To turn the purposes thou formest
Into fact.

Anonymous

I preach to you, then, that our country calls not for the life of ease, but for the life of strenuous endeavour. Let us therefore boldly face the life of strife, resolute to do our duty well; resolute to uphold righteousness by deed and by word; resolute to be both honest and brave, to serve high ideals, yet to use practical methods.

Theodore Roosevelt

One of Holman Hunt's pictures portrays an evening scene in the Carpenter's shop at Nazareth. Tools hang upon the walls; the floor is covered with shavings and chips; a rough wooden beam bears marks of the adze and saw. Jesus is standing near the door stretching himself after the day's toil, and the light of the setting sun falling on his outstretched arms throws on to the wall behind the shadow of a cross.

The cross . . . calls us to enter into the fellowship of Jesus' sufferings; to co-operate in his redemptive work; to live in dependence upon his grace; to offer ourselves a living sacrifice, holy, acceptable unto God.

Raymond Abba

Let there be love and understanding among us,
let peace and friendship be our shelter from life's
*   storms.*
Eternal God, help us to walk with good
*   companions,*
to live with hope in our hearts and eternity in our
*   thoughts,*
that we may lie down in peace and rise up
to find our hearts waiting to do your will.

Jewish prayer

I am a trapper* in the Gauber Pit. I have to trap without a light and I am scared. I go at four and sometimes half past three in the morning, and come out at five and half-past. I never go to sleep.

Sometimes I sing when I have light, but not in the dark; I dare not sing then. I don't like being in the pit.

* *A trapper opened and closed ventilation doors in a coal mine.*

Sarah Gooder
aged 8, Gauber Pit, West Yorkshire, 1842

While women weep, as they do now; I'll fight; while men go to prison, in and out, as they do now; I'll fight; while there is a drunkard left, while there is a poor lost girl upon the streets, where there remains one dark soul without the light of God – I'll fight! I'll fight to the very end!

William Booth

If I followed my own inclination I would sit in my armchair and take it easy for the rest of my life. But I dare not do it. I must work as long as life lasts.

Earl of Shaftesbury

His fourscore years have bent a back of oak,
His earth-brown cheeks are full of hollow pits;
His gnarled hands wander idly as he sits
Bending above the hearthstone's feeble smoke.
Threescore and ten slow years he tilled the land;
He wrung his bread out of the stubborn soil;
He saw his masters flourish through his toil;
He held their substance in his horny hand.

Now he is old: he asks for daily bread:
He who has sowed the bread he may not taste
Begs for crumbs: he would do no man wrong.
The Parish Guardians, when his case is read,
Will grant him, yet with no unseemly haste,
Just seventeen pence to starve on, seven days long.

Arthur Symons

It is true that missionaries have difficulties to encounter; but what great enterprise was ever accomplished without difficulty? For my part I have never ceased to rejoice that God has appointed me to such an office. People talk of the sacrifice I have made in spending so much of my time in Africa. Can that be called a sacrifice which simply paid back a small part of a great debt? It is emphatically no sacrifice. I know that in a few years I shall be cut off in that country. Do you carry on the work which I have begun. I leave it with you!

David Livingstone

No one is able to judge her own work – to know its value or its lack of value. Michelangelo wrote in his journal, 'I am a poor man of little value, who keeps striving in that art which God has given me, to lengthen my life as much as I can.' After his years of exhausting work on the Sistine vault he commented simply in a letter to his father: 'I've finished the chapel I was painting. The Pope is quite satisfied.'

Elizabeth O'Connor

At the end of life we will not be judged by
How many diplomas we have received
How much money we have made
How many great things we have done.

We will be judged by
I was hungry and you gave me to eat
I was naked and you clothed me
I was homeless and you took me in.

Mother Teresa

At the end of a busy day our minds are often filled with memories of activity and human encounters – exciting – boring – happy – distressing – special and ordinary. Even after a less active day we may be surprised at all that has happened to and around us.

Praying the day is rather like rerunning a film. We see a number of scenes, thoughts and actions on the screen of our mind. We do not stop to dwell on any of them for too long. We simply recognise and remember them – and finally, we offer up to God our day, such as it has been.

You may prefer to pray the day with your eyes closed. Some people find it more helpful to do it using pencil and paper. The important thing is that, once you have done it, you hand it over completely into God's keeping, and let go of it.

Cyril Skerratt

CONTRIBUTORS

Agatha Mary, SPB attended the Royal Holloway College and says that 'although my academic work was of a poor standard, I am grateful for the discipline of study that has remained with me'. Her first job was with Reuters, the news agency; her second with a unit of the International Missionary Council, (a precursor of the WCC), where she was involved with the writing, translation and production of books for African schools and colleges. Sister Agatha then spent 11 years as a missionary in Black urban areas of South Africa, following which she came to the Society of the Precious Blood at Burnham Abbey in Buckinghamshire.

Revd Alan Ashton is the Superintendent Minister of the Newmarket Circuit of the Methodist Church. Soham is one of 10 churches in the circuit. Alan left Wesley College, Bristol, in 1978 and has served in the Thetford, and Cromer & Sheringham Circuits. He holds strong commitments to issues surrounding peace in the Middle East, and often makes visits to the Land of the Holy One. A major hobby is flower arranging.

Dr Jill Brown qualified as a doctor in 1961 after studying in Cambridge and at St. Thomas's Hospital. She worked mainly in Community Child Health, especially with children with learning or developmental difficulties, or physical disability. After retiring Jill became involved with, and is now Chair of, the Peterborough Domestic Violence Forum, and she is also the Specialist Mission Networker for Domestic Violence for the Baptist Union.

Una Chandler was born in Barbados and came to Britain in 1962. She married in 1963, and has six children. She worked at her local school as a trained play worker until she recently gave it up to follow her calling as an Industrial Chaplain. A Methodist local preacher, in her spare time Una loves cooking, walking, and travelling around Britain.

Gillian Ellis has been a full-time freelance writer since 1989. She writes resource material for GirlGuiding UK and edits *The Trefoil*, the magazine for its senior section, the Trefoil Guild. Gillian also writes for the Scripture Union and for several newspapers and magazines, both Christian and secular. She is an enthusiastic member of the Association of Christian Writers and edits its in-house magazine, *Candle and Keyboard*. Gillian worships at an evangelical Anglican church, and she enjoys reading, singing, and travel.

Peter Garner is the Director of the Herefordshire Trade Federation, which incorporates the Herefordshire Christian Business Federation. The systematic study of the Scriptures (part of the training in evangelism which he joined after becoming a Christian) led him to study Christian Management Practice and its application to the working environment. The CHARISMA code, which Peter explains in his article, is the result of study and practical application, and its objective is to link and support working Christians throughout the UK.

Canon Dr Donald Gray, CBE was Rector of Liverpool before becoming a Canon of Westminster, Rector of St. Margaret's and Speaker's Chaplain in 1987. A historian and liturgist, he retired in 1998 and lives in Lincolnshire, where he continues to write. One of his books, *All Majesty and Power*, is a collection of prayers by and for royalty. He was for 20 years Chaplain to The Queen and was appointed a CBE in 1998.

Professor Peter Howdle began studying at the University of Leeds School of Medicine in 1966, and has spent most of his professional life there at St. James's University Hospital ('Jimmie's'). He is a Consultant Gastroenterologist and Professor in the Medical School. He has a large clinical practice, is responsible for the clinical training of medical students, and pursues his research interest in coeliac disease. Peter has been a local preacher since 1974, and from 2002-3 was Vice President of the Methodist Conference, completing a unique partnership since his wife, Susan, held that office from 1993-4.

191

Christine Kinch is a journalist with a regional newspaper in the *Birmingham Post and Mail* group. She is Local Preachers' Secretary in her local Methodist circuit, and a company director on a Regeneration Trust. One of her dreams is for racial integration in Britain. Her interests include the music of Purcell, Vaughan Williams and Frank Sinatra.

Graham Leighton has been truck driving for 39 years, and has had a PSV Double Decker Licence for 24 years. His longest trip was a drive across Europe to Bulgaria with his wife Jan, taking aid to an orphanage. Graham is currently Chairman of the CIRT, (Christians in Road Transport), which encourages anyone in transport to give their lives to God. Graham attends the Renewal Christian Centre, a multicultural church in Solihull.

Nigel Lightfoot formerly worked for the Methodist Publishing House, and is now a Funeral Director for the local Co-operative Funeral Service. He has held many offices within the Methodist Church, both at local church and circuit level, and he has also served on the General Committee of the Local Preachers Mutual Aid Association.

Dyfed Matthews is a retired Further Education Lecturer. He and his wife Anne spent five years in Tanzania where Dyfed was Head of Economics in a secondary school. Settling back in Britain in the 1970s Dyfed became a Further Education lecturer in Stoke and Colwyn Bay. Dyfed spends his retirement as a part-time piano technician and walking the dog! He is a member of Gideons International and also serves as a Deacon in a Baptist church.

Revd Tony Miles is a Methodist minister in the 15th year of ministry in Essex (currently Loughton; formerly Colchester). He presents a four-hour Saturday breakfast show for Premier Christian Radio. Together with his wife, Frances, and with help from their children, Hannah and Jonathan, he has published *Like a Child*, (available from Methodist Publishing House), a humorous devotional book encouraging people to open themselves to God's kingdom by listening to and observing children. These thoughts were originally broadcast between 1997-2002. Tony's other roles include being a chaplain to a NCH family centre, which will benefit from the sale of *Like a Child*.

Ken Russell began his working life in Liverpool, where he worked as an engineer on electronic telephone exchange design. A strong interest in music and sound reproduction led to his appointment as Technical Manager of a company making hi-fi equipment. When the company was later sold, he and his wife took on the management of a Christian Endeavour Guest House in North Wales. The influence of Christian Endeavour had led Ken to become a local preacher and he is currently Local Preachers' Secretary in the Colwyn Bay & Llandudno Circuit.

Cathy Sincock is the Artistic Director of the Springs Dance Company, which aims to communicate the Christian faith through dance.

Rt Hon Gary Streeter, MP was elected MP for Plymouth Sutton in 1992, after an earlier career in Law, and held a number of government posts in the Conservative administration. He became MP of the newly formed constituency of South West Devon in May 1997. Gary was appointed the Shadow Lord Chancellor's Department spokesman, and also became the Parliamentary Private Secretary to John Major, Leader of the Opposition. He has served as Shadow Minister for Europe and Shadow Secretary of State for International Development. From 2001-2 he was a Vice Chairman of the Conservative Party.
Details of 'Christians in Politics' can be found at www.christiansinpolitics.co.org

Brenda Thornton is an 'ordinary' member of the Methodist Church, and she has held office locally and connexionally. A teacher for 39 years, she retired in 1999.

Claire Wendelken held her first social work post with the Red Cross Family Support Service in Melbourne, Australia. She then worked for 25 years for an inner London Authority Social Services department, enabling children in care, their families and foster carers, developing policy and services for Under Fives and adults needing residential care. Claire was a tutor on an MSc Social Work course at the University of London for 20 years, and trained social services staff in two home counties and an outer London Borough. She is currently working with the Greater London Post Qualifying Consortium. She is a member of Queens Road Church, Wimbledon, and runs a group for senior citizens at New Malden Evangelical Free Church.

Social Workers' Christian Fellowship can be contacted through www.swcf.org.uk or by writing to SWCF c/o Truedata, 23 Park Road, Ilkeston, Derbyshire, DE7 5DA.

ACKNOWLEDGEMENTS

Methodist Publishing House gratefully acknowledges the use of copyright items. Every effort has been made to trace copyright owners, but where we have been unsuccessful we would welcome information which would enable us to make appropriate acknowledgement in any reprint.

Scripture quotations, unless otherwise stated, are from the New Revised Standard Version of the Bible, copyright 1989 by the Division of Christian Education of the National Council of Churches of Christ in the USA.

Page

12   Eric Milner-White, *My God, My Glory*, The Friends of York Minster.

14   'When you rise in the morning', *Celtic Parables*, ed. Robert van de Weyer, SPCK 1997, p.78. Permission applied for.

15   Henri Nouwen, *Behold the Beauty of the Lord: Praying with Icons*, Notre Dame/Ave Maria Press 1987, p.20-21.

22   Alan Sillitoe, 'Only the Lazy are Bored', *Echoes: Twenty-five years of the Telegraph Magazine*, W. H. Allen 1989, p.109-10.

23   Wendy M. Wright, *The Time Between, Cycles & Rhythms in Ordinary Time*, Upper Room Books 1999, p.181.

196

24   Paul Sangster, *Dr Sangster*, Epworth Press 1962, p.109.

33   William Barclay, *A Barclay Prayer Book,* 2nd edition, SCM Press 2003.

34   Ray Simpson, *Exploring Celtic Christianity,* Hodder & Stoughton 1995, p.62. Reproduced by permission of Hodder & Stoughton Limited.

36   Flora Thompson, *Lark Rise to Candleford,* Penguin.

45   James McGinnin, 'The Availability of Jesus', *Weavings,* Sep-Oct 1997, The Upper Room.

46   Rob Warner, *Walking with God*, Hodder & Stoughton 1998, p.153.

47   Elizabeth Goudge, *The Joy of the Snow*, Hodder & Stoughton 1977, p.18-19.

48   'Prayer from Canada', *A Procession of Prayers, Prayers & Meditations from around the world,* comp. John Carden. Council of Churches for Britain and Ireland, Week of Prayer for Christian Unity 1991.

48   Gordon Macdonald, *Ordering your Private World*, Highland Books, p.74-5.

56   Carlo Carretto, *Letters from the Desert*, Darton, Longman & Todd.

56   Kahlil Gibran, *The Prophet*, Alfred Knopf Inc. Permission applied for.

57   Clifford Smith, *Waterways World*, September 1992, p.58.

71   Thomas R. Hawkins, *The Potter & the Clay*, Upper Room Books.

72   Vera Brittain, *Testament of Youth*, Fontana Paperbacks 1979, p.240.

73   David Winter, *What's in a Word?* Bible Reading Fellowship, 1994, p.131.

75   James A. Michener, *Hawaii*, Corgi Books 1987, p.620.

84   Basil Hume, *To be a Pilgrim*, Triangle/SPCK 1999, p.205.

86   'Kenya', *A Procession of Prayers, Prayers & Meditations from around the world*, comp. John Carden. *Prayers for Today*: Uzima Press (Imami House, St. John's Gate, PO Box 48127) Nairobi.

94   Jean Coggan, *Pearls of Wisdom*, ed. Wendy Wilson, Darton, Longman & Todd 1988, p.37.

95   Robert G. Twycross, *A Time to Die*, Christian Medical Fellowship, 1984.

97   John Polkinghorne, *Searching for Truth – A Scientist looks at the Bible*, Bible Reading Fellowship 1996, p.64-5.

103   'Lord, you have come', David Jenkins. Permission applied for.

104   Esther de Waal, *The Celtic Way of Prayer*, Hodder & Stoughton, 1996, p.70.

105   Avery Brooke, 'Running out of Time', *Weavings*, May-June 1998, The Upper Room.

114   Susan Howatch, *Sweet Inspiration*, introduced by Alan Titchmarsh, ed. Anuradha Vittachi, Hodder & Stoughton 1994, p.71.

114   Cicely Saunders, *Sweet Inspiration*, introduced by Alan Titchmarsh, ed. Anuradha Vittachi, Hodder & Stoughton 1994, p.126.

115   Agatha Christie, *An Autobiography*, William Collins & Sons Ltd.

116   Iris Murdoch, *The Bell*, Chatto & Windus.

116   Catherine Bramwell-Booth, *Letters*, Lion Publishing 1986, p.18.

123   Michel Quoist, *The Christian Response*, Gill and Son, Dublin 1975.

123   Toyohiko Kagawa, *New Life through God*, Baker Book House.

124   Joan Clifford, *The Mellow Years,* Foundery Press.

125   W. Paul Jones, *The Province beyond the River*, Upper Room Books 1981, p.41.

126   John Pollock, *John Wesley*, Lion Publishing 1989, p.239.

127   Rowland Parker, *The Common Stream*, Paladin 1979, p.59.

127   Edward Storey, *Portrait of the Fen Country*, Robert Hale 1971, p.30.

134   'They who tread the path of labour', Henry van Dyke, Charles Scribners' Sons. Permission applied for.

143   'Father, source of all power', Caryl Micklem, ed., *Contemporary Prayers: The Collected Edition*, SCM Press 1993.

144   John Baillie, *A Diary of Private Prayer*, Oxford University Press. Permission applied for.

145   Ramon Huston, *Order! Order!*, Marshalls Paperbacks 1981.

146   'You asked for my hands', Joe Seremane/Christian Aid. Permission applied for.

155   Lord Hailsham, *The Door Wherein I Went*, William Collins 1975, p.184.

156-7 'Lord, I get so busy', Eddie Askew, *A Silence and A Shouting*, The Leprosy Mission International, 80 Windmill Road, Brentford, Middlesex TW8 0QH.

158 'A Muslim's first prayer as a Christian'; 'Prayer of a Ghanaian harbour man out of work', *The Oxford Book of Prayer*, p.88/101, Oxford University Press. Permission applied for.

159 Elizabeth J. Canham, *Heart Whispers, Benedictine Wisdom for Today*, Upper Room Books 1999, p.92.

164 Robert Corin Morris, *Wrestling with Grace*, Upper Room Books 2003, p.61-2.

165 Winifred Holtby, *South Riding*, Fontana Paperbacks, p.27.

166 'Creator of Rainbows', Kate McIlhagga, *The Book of Christian Prayer*, SPCK. Permission applied for.

167 Leslie Weatherhead, *Psychology and Life*, Hodder & Stoughton, p.204-5.

173 E. Jack Mitchell, *A Cornishman Remembers*, Campaign Literature 1991, p.45.

174 Anthony Hulbert, *Contours of God from Old Testament Stories*, Canterbury Press.

175 Roger Nowell and Jeremy Mills, *The Skipper, A Fisherman's Tale*, BBC 1993, p.48.

176 James Jones, *People of the Blessing*, Bible Reading Fellowship 1998, p.134.

176 Gormola Kernewek, *The Celtic Heart*, ed. Pat Robson, HarperCollins p.170.

177 Delia Smith, *A Journey into God*, Spire/Hodder & Stoughton 1990, p.148.

177   Marva J. Dawn, *To Walk and Not Faint, A Month of Meditations on Isaiah 40*, Wm. B. Eerdmans Publishing Co. 1997.

184   Raymond Abba, *Things Which Abide*, Epworth Press.

186   Arthur Symons, 'The Old Labourer', *The Poems of Arthur Symons*, by permission of Brian Read.

187   Elizabeth O'Connor, *Cry Pain, Cry Hope*, The Servant Leadership School, 1640 Columbia Road NW, Washington DC 20009, USA, in Francis Dewar, *Invitations, God's Calling for Everyone*, SPCK 1996.

187   Mother Teresa, *Words to Love By*, Notre Dame: Ave Maria Press. Permission applied for.

188   Cyril Skerratt, *Exploring Prayer*, Methodist Publishing House.